A People's History for the Classroom

Bill Bigelow

The Zinn Education Project

A collaboration between Rethinking Schools and Teaching for Change

A People's History for the Classroom
by Bill Bigelow

A Rethinking Schools Publication

Rethinking Schools, Ltd., is a nonprofit educational publisher of books, booklets, and a quarterly magazine on school reform, with a focus on issues of equity and social justice. To request additional copies of this book or a catalog of other publications, or to subscribe to *Rethinking Schools* magazine, contact:
Rethinking Schools
1001 East Keefe Avenue
Milwaukee, Wisconsin 53212
800-669-4192
www.rethinkingschools.org

Teaching for Change provides teachers and parents the tools to transform schools into socially equitable centers of learning. Its resources include professional development, publications, and a catalog of progressive teaching materials. For more information or a copy of the Teaching for Change catalog, contact:
Teaching for Change
P.O. Box 73038
Washington, D.C. 20056
800-763-9131
www.teachingforchange.org

© 2008 Rethinking Schools, Ltd.
First edition

Cover Design: MJ Karp
Book Design: Kate Hawley
Proofreading: Jennifer Morales
Business Manager: Mike Trokan
Front cover photo: Lawrence Strike, 1912, © Brown Brothers, Sterling PA
Back cover photo: Anti-lynching protest, NYC, 1917, © Underwood & Underwood, NY. Library of Congress.

ISBN: 978-0-942961-39-3

Table of Contents

191041

Preface

IN LATE 2007, A FORMER BOSTON UNIVERSITY student watched *You Can't Be Neutral on a Moving Train*, the film about the life of historian, professor, and activist Howard Zinn. He recalled attending Professor Zinn's remarkable lectures at BU in the 1970s, and marveled at how Zinn's "people's history" was so much more alive and accurate than the traditional history he'd received in high school.

Now, after a successful career in technology, he wanted to contribute to bringing Zinn's work to a new generation of students. So he contacted Howard Zinn who put him in touch with Rethinking Schools and Teaching for Change, both non-profit organizations, each with over 20 years of experience in providing social justice resources and professional development for pre-K-12 classroom teachers and teacher educators.

"I'd prefer to remain anonymous," he told us. "This is not about me; it's about getting Howard Zinn's work into the hands of as many teachers as possible."

So with the generous support of this anonymous donor, Rethinking Schools and Teaching for Change have partnered to produce and offer a unique educational packet, which includes the DVD *You Can't Be Neutral on a Moving Train*, about Howard Zinn's life; Howard Zinn's classic text, *A People's History of the United States*; and a teaching guide, assembled especially for this project. We are promoting and distributing the packets nationally to middle and high school teachers, while supplies last. A dedicated webpage, www.ZinnEdProject.org, provides additional recommended resources and ongoing updates about the project and its impact. The film and book are also commercially available, and additional copies of the teaching guide can be downloaded for free from the website or ordered from either Rethinking Schools or Teaching for Change.

A note about this teaching guide. As explained in the introduction, the activities included here are designed to offer curriculum ideas to complement Howard Zinn's history. Some of the articles and lessons—most of which first appeared in *Rethinking Schools* magazine or books—are pegged directly to Zinn's work; others deal with themes and episodes that Zinn addresses. This guide is a sampler. Many more "people's history" curriculum books are available from Rethinking Schools and Teaching for Change.

Some 30 years after his exposure to Howard Zinn's approach to history, the former Boston University student who triggered this project demonstrates that classroom experience can have a lifelong impact. We believe that through taking a more engaging and more honest look at the past, we can help equip students with the analytical tools to make sense of—and improve—the world today.

—Rethinking Schools and
Teaching for Change

Introduction:
A People's History, A People's Pedagogy

THE LAST TIME HOWARD ZINN CAME TO speak in Portland, Ore., where I've taught high school history since 1978, hundreds of people packed the auditorium to hear him. Those unable to find seats stood throughout the hall; others sat on the floor or crowded onto the stage. Hundreds more were turned away, unable to squeeze in. A colleague at my high school said, only half in jest, that it was one of the saddest days of his life, not being able to get in to hear Howard Zinn.

Something unusual is going on when a historian draws crowds like a rock star.

Unusual, but not surprising. Zinn's *people's* history is passionate, probing, and partisan. Zinn begins from the premise that the lives of ordinary people matter—that history ought to focus on those who too often receive only token attention (workers, women, people of color), and also on how people's actions, individually and collectively, shaped our society. And it's a people's history in that it's a perspective on the past that is usable today, that can instruct and inspire and caution as we try to make the world a better place.

Contrast Zinn's approach with a traditional textbook history. As anyone who has ever cracked a history textbook can affirm, they're boring. The prose reads like words and ideas have first been run through a blender. Passionless, story-poor, the books feign Objectivity. There is a lot of "us," and "we," and "our," as if the texts are trying to dissolve

Jordin Isip

1

race, class, and gender realities into the melting pot of "the nation." Indeed, the books have titles like *The Rise of the American Nation*, embracing a curricular manifest destiny where all history led gloriously (or by about page 700, tediously) to Us.

Zinn's writing presents no such illusions. In fact, the title of his autobiography (and the film distributed by the Zinn Education Project) insists: *You Can't Be Neutral on a Moving Train.* Societies are dynamic, conflict-ridden, with power played out in every aspect of life. Historians cannot remain outside or "above" these struggles, Zinn argues. None of us can. Our lives, our occupations, our consumer choices—and, yes, how we tell history—all take sides, and help move the world in one direction or another.

"Anyone reading history should understand from the start that there is no such thing as impartial history," Zinn writes in a book of essays, *Declarations of Independence.* "All written history is partial in two senses. It is partial in that it is only a tiny part of what really happened. That is a limitation that can never be overcome. And it is partial in that it inevitably takes sides, by what it includes or omits, what it emphasizes or deemphasizes. It may do this openly or deceptively, consciously or subconsciously."

The textbooks most of us have read as students or have been assigned to teach throughout our careers do not acknowledge their biases. As Zinn suggests, the authors may even be unaware of them. The most recent history textbook I was assigned in Portland, *American Odyssey* (Glencoe) describes the U.S. War with Mexico in two bland paragraphs, out of its 1,010 pages (see p. 49). It never mentions widespread U.S. opposition to the war at the time. It was during this war that Henry David Thoreau went to jail and coined the term "civil disobedience," in defense of his refusal to pay taxes to support U.S. aggression against Mexico. Today, as the United States wages two wars in foreign lands and engages in military actions in many more, isn't a textbook biased when it fails to alert

students to the long antiwar and anti-imperialist traditions in our country's history? And with so much conversation about "protecting our borders," isn't it biased not to explore where those borders came from in the first place?

In the first chapter of *A People's History of the United States,* Zinn notes how so much history-telling concentrates on those at the top—the presidents and diplomats, the generals and industrialists. It's a winner's history, and implicitly tells students: Pay attention to the victors and disregard the rest. Zinn flips the script, as the kids say. He writes that, "I prefer to try to tell the story of the discovery of America from the viewpoint of the Arawaks, of the Constitution from the standpoint of the

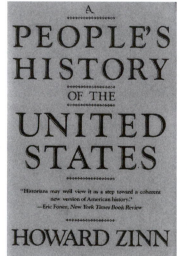

slaves, of Andrew Jackson as seen by the Cherokees, of the Civil War as seen by the New York Irish, of the Mexican War as seen by the deserting soldiers of Scott's army, of the rise of industrialism as seen by the young women in the Lowell textile mills, of the Spanish-American war as seen by the Cubans, the conquest of the Philippines as seen by the black soldiers on Luzon, the Gilded Age as seen by southern farmers, the First World War as seen by socialists, the Second World War as seen by pacifists, the New Deal as seen by blacks in Harlem, the postwar American empire as seen by peons in Latin America."

This from-the-grassroots, people's history is grounded in Zinn's own experiences: "Before I became a professional historian, I had grown up in the dirt and dankness of New York tenements, had been knocked unconscious by a policeman while holding a banner in a demonstration, had worked for three years in a shipyard, and had participated in the violence of war."

But Zinn's approach to history is not simply a personal preference based on his own experiences. When we look at history from the standpoint of the workers and not just the owners, the soldiers and not just the generals, the invaded and not just the invaders, we can begin to see society more fully, more accurately. So often, history books describe a flattened world of "U.S. interests" and generic Americans. As Zinn writes, "Nations are not communities and never have been. The history of any country, presented as the history of a family, conceals fierce conflicts of interest (sometimes exploding, most often repressed) between conquerors and conquered, masters and slaves, capitalists and workers, dominators and dominated in race and sex." Zinn recognizes that we live with the consequences of these fierce conflicts of interest today. Thus the more clearly we see the past, the more clearly we'll see the present—and be equipped to improve it.

None of this is to argue for a history that exaggerates the crimes of the powerful, inflates the heroism of "the people," or invents victories for social movements. But history-writing that begins with a belief in the possibility of a fundamentally egalitarian society will necessarily make alternative selections from our nation's past. Zinn's commitments and work in civil rights and peace movements have led him to propose that history be put to the service of working and teaching for a better world. History is about and for human beings.

Commitment and justice, critique and hope. It seems to me that it's all of this that draws people—and especially teachers—to Howard Zinn's scholarship. I know that early in my career, this is what drew me to Zinn's work.

A People's Pedagogy

A people's history requires a people's pedagogy to match. The activities included in this booklet are not a chapter-by-chapter guide to Zinn's *A People's History of the United States*. Instead, they feature teaching strategies that illustrate how a people's history can be brought to life in the classroom.

A fundamental problem with traditional history *and* with traditional history teaching is that it can appear that each event leads inexorably to the next: this happened then this happened then

this happened, like dominoes lined up and falling. Social changes can seem almost inevitable. Laid out in neatly sequenced chapters, textbooks present social reality as if it were unfolding rather than being created by people. As Zinn writes in his autobiography: "Everything in history once it has happened looks as if it had to happen exactly that way. We can't imagine any other. But I am convinced of the uncertainty of history, of the possibility of surprise, of the importance of human action in changing what looks unchangeable."

Zinn proposes history as a series of choices and turning points—junctures at which ordinary people interpreted social conditions and took actions that made a difference. This is a powerful and hopeful insight that can not only help our students think about the present, but can empower them to act on it. What we think and how we act can make the world a better place. For teachers, our challenge is how to bring this insight alive in our classrooms—not just *telling* students this, but *showing* them. Role plays are one teaching strategy that can bring history-making to life in the classroom. Role plays ask students to attempt to imagine themselves in the circumstances of other individuals throughout history and to consider the choices that actual groups faced.

For example, because of the enormity of slavery, it may appear to students that its abolition was foreordained. But this misses the significance of the social movement that sought to end slavery, its difficult choices, and the breadth of resistance, beginning especially with the enslaved themselves, that ultimately brought slavery down. I ask my students how many of them—were they transported to, say, 1850, with their current awareness intact—would have opposed slavery. Of course, they all raise their hands. Then I ask, "What would you have done about it?" Not so many hands raised. In a role play, I ask all my students to portray members of the American Anti-Slavery Society, a key abolitionist organization. In role, they confront dilemmas that anti-slavery

A people's history can instruct and inspire and caution as we try to make the world a better place.

organizers also encountered: Would they have maintained a singular focus on slavery in the South or would they have spent their energies also opposing racism in the North? Would they have supported the Seneca Falls gathering by women's rights advocates, many of them abolitionists, or do they think this would have divided the movement? How would they have confronted the 1850 Fugitive Slave Act? Would they have supported John Brown with money and weapons? None of these are easy strategic questions and as students debate these they can more easily recognize that, in fact, people *do* make history. Choices are made in circumstances not of their making, but nonetheless how people analyze and decide to act within those circumstances influences the course of events.

The Bread and Roses Strike role play, included in this guide, is structured similarly, and puts students in the position of Industrial Workers of the World (IWW) organizers in Lawrence, Mass., in 1912, who attempt to unite over 20,000 immigrant workers, speaking dozens of languages, for wage increases and better conditions—for "bread." But they also seek "roses." It's a strike about dignity. Ultimately, organizers hope to "win" workers' commitment to a more democratic society and non-exploitative economic system. Here, too, students experience classroom doses of the actual historical participants' confusion, frustration, but also solidarity. And, here too, there was no inevitability about the outcome, as students readily grasp from the difficulty of the choices they confront in their role as IWW organizers. Role plays like this one and on the Abolition movement are components of a pedagogy that does not merely *tell* students that people make history, but seeks to let them live that insight in the classroom.

Another piece of a "people's pedagogy" is that it should engage students in explicitly critiquing

Zinn begins from the premise that the lives of ordinary people matter—that history ought to focus on those who too often receive only token attention (workers, women, people of color), and also on how people's actions, individually and collectively, shaped our society.

traditional approaches to history—including their own textbooks. In one article included here, I describe how I introduce my classes to the problematic notion of Columbus's "discovery of America": I steal a student's purse (see p. 15). I do everything I can to get students to agree with me that "Nomika's" purse is in fact my purse: I demonstrate that I control it; I take items out and claim them (Nomika has been alerted in advance, but other students don't know that), and I insist that it is my purse. When I lose this argument with the class, I offer to "recast the act of purse acquisition," and tell students that I didn't steal Nomika's purse, I *discovered* it. Now it's mine, right? Students readily see the shoddiness of the claim. "So," I ask them, "if I didn't discover Nomika's purse, then why do some people say that Columbus discovered America? What are some other terms that we could use to describe his actions?" He stole America; he took it; he ripped it off; he invaded it. In a five- or ten-minute simulation, students can begin to see what Howard Zinn argues throughout his work: that how we frame the past invariably takes sides. And when we use terms like "discovery"—or even the seemingly more neutral "encounter"—our language sides with the ones who came out on top.

Because the combination of a people's history with a people's pedagogy may bump up against students' prior notions of what ought to happen in a history class, it's helpful to engage students in comparisons that call into question traditional approaches. For example, one activity included here is "The U.S.-Mexican War Tea Party (p. 29)," pegged to Chapter 8 of *A People's History of the United States*, "We Take Nothing By Conquest, Thank God." This was the war that resulted in Mexico ceding about half its country to the United States, including California, Arizona, New Mexico, and Texas. In the "tea party" role play, students assume the personas of 21 individuals, all of whom had some connection to the U.S. war with Mexico (1846-1848): the abolitionist Frederick Douglass opposed the war because he saw it as an attempt to add more slave territory to the United States; Jefferson Davis, of Mississippi, too, saw this as an issue of slavery—expanding his "freedom" to take his slaves wherever he wanted; María Josefa Martínez, of Santa Fe, New Mexico, feared losing her land and rights, that were protected more under Mexican law than under U.S. law; Sergeant John Riley, originally of Ireland, deserted the U.S. Army, where he and other immigrants received wretched treatment, and joined the Mexicans to form the Saint Patrick's Battalion; Col. Ethan Allan Hitchcock of the U.S. Army saw the war as an attempt to steal huge swaths of Mexico, and wrote that "My heart is not in this war," but as a military officer was pledged to carry out his orders; and the Apache leader, Cochise, condemns both the U.S. and Mexico as thieves, fighting amongst themselves for land that doesn't belong to either of them. Portraying these and 15 others, students meet one another to find individuals who support the war, oppose the war, stand to lose or gain from the war, and who have opinions on why the war was fought.

> *When we use terms like "discovery"—or even the seemingly more neutral "encounter"—our language sides with the ones who came out on top.*

The activity, which takes about a class period, exposes students to a much more diverse range of perspectives on the war than they'd find in any textbook. But I don't want students to take my word for that; I want to "argue" for this kind of historical and pedagogical approach by allowing them to compare it to their own textbook: Glencoe's *American Odyssey*, mentioned earlier. Whereas in the tea party, students encountered over 20 different perspectives on the war—Mexican, U.S., men, women, pro-war, anti-war, pro-slavery, abolitionist, wealthy, poor, white, black, Native American, soldier, civilian— their book includes three perspectives: white

Southerners, Northerners, and Mexico (as in: "Mexico was outraged …").

I ask students to read their textbook's "War with Mexico" section and to reflect in writing on the adequacy of the book's treatment, what's left out, and whether or not they think it makes any difference that this is all some students will learn about the war with Mexico. After the tea party and reading Zinn's chapter, students offer a rich critique of their textbook. Not only do students readily note the missing perspectives, they also spot things that are less obvious. As Katie said in our discussion, "We're not asked to think about whether or not the war is right." Another student noted how the passage desensitizes readers to the meaning of war: "It doesn't even look at it as a war—it's a situation." In fact, despite the section's title, "War with Mexico," the first paragraph ends with May 1846 and the second paragraph begins with February 2, 1848, entirely skipping the war itself. Another student underlined how the book says that the Treaty of Guadalupe Hidalgo "gave the United States vast new regions …": "'Gave.' This makes it sound all legal."

An activity like this allows students to see how much richer and more accurate a "people's history" is than the traditional approach, as exemplified by their textbook. A people's history (and a people's pedagogy) doesn't silence the perspectives of the elites, it simply includes more voices in the conversation. And a people's pedagogy offers students a different, more participatory, relationship to text. The traditional curriculum treats students as word consumers: read this and answer the questions at the end of the chapter. A more critical approach encourages students to "talk back" to text, to read for the silences and the neglected perspectives, to ask why certain choices were made (for example, why the text included no mention of the large numbers of Mexico war opponents), and to imagine what a more adequate treatment would be. In this respect, reading is a metaphor: when we ask students to evaluate text material for biases, implicitly we're inviting them to evaluate the larger society for biases. A people's pedagogy seeks to nurture active citizens, rather than consumers.

In his article, "Unsung Heroes," included in this teaching guide (p. 51), Howard Zinn acknowledges that once we begin to teach a fuller, more honest history, we also begin to surface the exploitation and brutality that has often been glossed over in the traditional history curriculum. Zinn writes: "A high school student recently confronted me: 'I read in your book *A People's History of the United States* about the massacres of Indians, the long history of racism, the persistence of poverty in the richest country in the world, the senseless wars. How can I keep from being thoroughly alienated and depressed?'"

This disillusion that we're confronted with is magnified because so much traditional history manipulates students to see the policies of the U.S. government as our policies. Of course, it's not just textbooks that lead us to identify with government and military actions. Here's Barbara Walters anchoring *ABC News* during the first Gulf War: "How does this change our strategy? This means we can't bomb; it means we have to be very careful about the areas we attack, if we do

attack." (The media watchdog group Fairness and Accuracy in Reporting calls this the "we we" phenomenon.) This is not a liberal-conservative thing; the most liberal commentators adopt this linguistic practice of conflating our interests with those of the elites.

No wonder then, that when students begin to see the reality behind corporate and government policies, they may take this personally and become discouraged or defensive. But a people's pedagogy, like a people's history, should not be one long story of brutality and exploitation. Several activities in this guide alert students to deep currents of justice and equality in U.S. history, and in diverse ways encourage students to try on the personas of people who worked to make this a more democratic society. A people's history and pedagogy ought to allow students to recognize that "we" were not necessarily the ones stealing land, dropping bombs, or breaking strikes. "We" were ending slavery, fighting for women's rights, organizing unions, marching against wars, and trying to create a society premised on the Golden Rule.

The article in this teaching guide that follows Zinn's "Unsung Heroes," "Teaching Unsung Heroes," also begins with a tea party that introduces students to over 30 individuals in U.S.

United Farm Workers leader César Chávez addresses union supporters in Los Angeles in 1976.

history who worked for "racial and gender justice." Students portray some well-known activists like Rosa Parks and César Chávez, and some less well-known activists like Harvey Milk, Fred Korematsu, and Elaine Brown. Students-as-activists search out individuals who "spent time in jail for their activities or beliefs," "worked for women's rights, workers' rights, or for the rights of gays and lesbians," and "worked against slavery or other forms of racism." They find people who rejected violence on principle and others (like John Brown) who saw violence as the only way to stop a much greater violence. And from this initial tea party they choose individuals to research and write about imaginatively—in story, dialogue, or interior monologue. I include some examples from student papers in "Teaching Unsung Heroes."

One of the remarkable things about Howard Zinn's scholarship is his capacity to narrate stories that are often unbelievably horrific and yet never lose sight of the goodness that courses through human experience. Zinn's history is both more honest than traditional histories but also more hopeful.

In the wake of September 11th, Rethinking Schools editors searched for writing that could help us make sense out of what our society—and what the world—was going through. One passage that we turned to was the concluding paragraphs of Zinn's autobiography, *You Can't Be Neutral on a Moving Train.* It's about life, but it's also about what we need to strive for in our curricula:

"To be hopeful in bad times is not just foolishly romantic. It is based on the fact that human history is a history not only of cruelty, but also of compassion, sacrifice, courage, kindness.

"What we choose to emphasize in this complex history will determine our lives. If we see only the worst, it destroys our capacity to do something. If we remember those times and places—and there are so many—where people have behaved magnificently, this gives us the energy to act, and at least the possibility of sending this spinning top of a world in a different direction.

"And if we do act, in however small a way, we don't have to wait for some grand utopian future. The future is an infinite succession of presents, and to live *now* as we think human beings should live, in defiance of all that is bad around us, is itself a marvelous victory."

I see Howard Zinn's work as an invitation to us all to join our classrooms to that "infinite succession of presents"—to see our work with students not only in terms of teaching academic skills, but also in terms of building a just society. ■

Civil rights activists march across the Edmund Pettus Bridge, Montgomery, Ala., March 9, 1965.

Why Students Should Study History

An Interview with Howard Zinn

The following is condensed from an interview with Howard Zinn. He was interviewed in 1994 by Barbara Miner of Rethinking Schools *magazine.*

Why should students study history?

I started studying history with one view in mind: to look for answers to the issues and problems I saw in the world about me. By the time I went to college I had worked in a shipyard, had been in the Air Force, had been in a war. I came to history asking questions about war and peace, about wealth and poverty, about racial division.

Sure, there's a certain interest in inspecting the past and it can be fun, sort of like a detective story. I can make an argument for knowledge for its own sake as something that can add to your life. But while that's good, it is small in relation to the very large objective of trying to understand and do something about the issues that face us in the world today.

Students should be encouraged to go into history in order to come out of it, and should be discouraged from going into history and getting lost in it, as some historians do.

What do you see as some of the major problems in how U.S. history has been taught in this country?

One major problem has been the intense focus on U.S. history in isolation from the world. This is a

Roslyn Zinn

problem that all nations have, their nationalistic focus on their own history, and it goes to absurd lengths. Some states in this country even require a yearlong course in the history of that state.

But even if you are willing to see the United States in relation to world history, you face the problem that we have not looked at the world in an equitable way. We have concentrated on the Western world, in fact on Western Europe. I remember coming into my first class in Spelman College in Atlanta in 1956 and finding that there was no required course in black history, or Asian or African history, but there was a required course in the history of England. And there on the board was this chart of the Tudors and the Stuarts, the dynasties of England.

For the United States, emphasis has been particularly glaring in terms of Latin America, which is that part of the world closest to us and with which we've had the most to do economically and politically.

Another glaring problem has been the emphasis in teaching American history through the eyes of the important and powerful people, through the presidents, the Congress, the Supreme Court, the generals, the industrialists. History textbooks don't say, "We are going to tell the story of the Mexican War from the standpoint of the generals," but when they tell us it was a great military victory, that's exactly what they are doing.

Taking that as an example, if one were to have a more inclusive view of the war with Mexico, what would be some of the themes and perspectives one would include?

The Mexican War is an example of how one event raises so many issues. You'd have to see the war first of all as more than a military action. So often the history of war is dominated by the story of battles, and this is a way of diverting attention from the political factors behind a war. It's possible to concentrate upon the battles of the Mexican War and just to talk about the triumphant march into Mexico City, and not talk about the relationship of the Mexican War to slavery and to the acquisition of territories which might possibly be slave territories.

Another thing that is neglected in the Mexican War is the viewpoint of the ordinary soldiers. The soldiers who had volunteered for the Mexican War—you didn't need a draft because so many people in the working classes were so destitute that they would join the military on the promise of a little bit of pay and mustering-out money and a little bit of prestige—the volunteers went into it not really knowing the bloodshed it would involve. And then so many of them deserted. For example, seven regiments of General Winfield Scott deserted on the road to Mexico City.

You should tell the story of the Massachusetts volunteers who went into the Mexican War. Half of them died, and the half who returned were invited to a homecoming party and when a commanding officer got up to address the gathering, they booed him off the platform.

I think it's a good idea also to do something which isn't done anywhere so far as I know in histories in any country, and that is: tell the story of the war from the standpoint of the other side, of "the enemy." To tell the story of the Mexican War from the standpoint of the Mexicans means to ask:

So often the history of war is dominated by the story of battles, and this is a way of diverting attention from the political factors behind a war.

How did they feel about having 40 percent of their territory taken away from them as a result of the war? How did they view the incident that President Polk used as a reason for the beginning of the war? Did it look real or manufactured to them?

You'd also have to talk about the people in the United States who protested against the war. That would be the time to bring up Henry Thoreau and his essay, "Civil Disobedience."

You'd have to look at Congress and how it behaved. You'd have to look at Abraham Lincoln, who was in the House of Representatives during the Mexican War. You'd learn a lot about politicians and politics because you'd see that Abraham Lincoln on the one hand spoke up against the war, but on the other hand voted to give money to finance the war. This is so important because this is something that is repeated again and again in American history: the feeble opposition in Congress to presidential wars, and then the voting of funds for whatever war the President has initiated.

How do you prevent history lessons from becoming a recitation of dates and battles and Congresspersons and presidents?

You can take any incident in American history and enrich it and find parallels with today. One important thing is not to concentrate on chronological order, but to go back and forth and find similarities and analogies.

You should ask students if anything in a particular historical event reminds them of something they read in the newspapers or see on television about the world today. When you press students to make connections, to abstract from the uniqueness of a particular historical event and find something it has in common with another event—then history becomes alive, not just past but present.

And, of course, you must raise the controversial questions and ask students, "Was it right for us to take Mexican territory? Should we be proud of that; should we celebrate that?" History teachers often think they must avoid judgments of right and wrong because, after all, those are matters of subjective opinions, those are issues on which students will disagree and teachers will disagree.

But it's the areas of disagreement that are the most important. Questions of right and wrong and justice are exactly the questions that should be raised all the time. When students are asked, "Is this right; is this wrong?" then it becomes interesting, then they can have a debate—especially if they learn that there's no simple, absolute, agreed-upon, universal answer. It's not like giving them multiple-choice questions where they are right or wrong. I think that's a tremendous advance in their understanding of what education is.

Teachers must also address the problem that people have been miseducated to become dependent on government, to think that their supreme act as citizens is to go to the polls and vote every two years or four years. That's where the history of social movements comes in. Teachers should dwell on Shay's Rebellion, on colonial rebellions, on the abolitionist movement, on the populist movement, on the labor movement, and so on, and make sure these social movements don't get lost in the overall story of presidents and Congresses and Supreme Courts. Emphasizing social and protest movements in the making of history gives students a feeling that they as citizens are the most important actors in history.

Students, for example, should learn that during the Depression there were strikes and demonstrations all over the country. And it was that turmoil and protest that created the atmosphere in which Roosevelt and Congress passed Social Security and unemployment insurance and housing subsidies and so on.

How can teachers foster critical thinking so that students don't merely memorize a new, albeit more progressive, set of facts?

Substituting one indoctrination for another is a danger and it's very hard to deal with. After all, the teacher, no matter how hard she or he tries, is the dominant figure in the classroom and has the power of authority and of grades. It's easy for the teacher to fall into the trap of bullying students into accepting one set of facts or ideas. It takes hard work and delicate dealings with students to overcome that.

The way I've tried to deal with that problem is to make it clear to the students that when we study history we are dealing with controversial issues with no one, absolute, god-like answer. And that I, as a teacher, have my opinion and they

Police escort a group of black children to jail in Birmingham, Ala. on May 4, 1963. They were among the more than 900 children arrested for protesting the city's segregation laws.

can have their opinions, and that I, as a teacher, will try to present as much information as I can but that I may leave out information. I try to make them understand that while there are experts on facts, on little things, on the big issues, on the controversies and the issues of right and wrong and justice, there are no experts, and their opinion is as good as mine.

But how do you then foster a sense of justice and avoid the trap of relativity that, "Well, some people say this and some people say that"?

I find such relativity especially true on the college level, where there's a great tendency to indecisiveness. People are unwilling to take a stand on a moral issue because, well, there's this side and there's that side.

I deal with this by example. I never simply present both sides and leave it at that. I take a stand. If I'm dealing with Columbus, I say, look, there are these people who say that we shouldn't judge Columbus by the standards of the 20th century. But my view is that basic moral standards are not different for the 20th century or the 15th century.

I don't simply lay history out on a platter and say, "I don't care what you choose; they're both valid." I let them know, "No, I care what you choose; I don't think they're both valid. But you don't have to agree with me." I want them to know that if people don't take a stand the world will remain unchanged, and who wants that?

Are there specific ways that teachers can foster an anti-racist perspective?

To a great extent, this moral objective is not considered in teaching history. I think people have to be given the facts of slavery, the facts of racial segregation, the facts of government complicity in racial segregation, the facts of the fight for equality. But that is not enough.

I think students need to be aroused emotionally on the issue of equality. They have to try to feel what it was like, to be a slave, to be jammed into slave ships, to be separated from your family. Novels, poems, autobiographies, memoirs, the reminiscences of ex-slaves, the letters that slaves wrote, the writings of Frederick Douglass—I think they have to be introduced as much as possible. Students should learn the words of people themselves, to feel their anger, their indignation.

In general, I don't think there has been enough use of literature in history. People should read Richard Wright's *Black Boy*; they should read the poems of Countee Cullen; they should read the

Feminists march on August 26, 1970, the 50th anniversary of women's suffrage, in a nationwide "strike for equality" called by the National Organization for Women.

novels of Alice Walker, the poems of Langston Hughes, Lorraine Hansbury's *A Raisin in the Sun*. These writings have an emotional impact that can't be found in an ordinary recitation of history.

It is especially important that students learn about the relationship of the United States government to slavery and race.

It's very easy to fall into the view that slavery and racial segregation were a Southern problem. The federal government is very often exempted from responsibility for the problem, and is presented as a benign force helping black people on the road to equality. In our time, students are taught how Eisenhower sent his troops to Little Rock, Ark., and Kennedy sent troops to Oxford, Miss., and Congress passed civil rights laws.

Yet the federal government is very often an obstacle to resolving those problems of race, and when it enters it comes in late in the picture. Abraham Lincoln was not the initiator of the movement against slavery but a follower of a movement that had developed for 30 years by the time he became president in 1861; it was the antislavery movement that was the major force creating the atmosphere in which emancipation took place following the Civil War. And it was the president and Congress and the Supreme Court that ignored the 13th, 14th, and 15th Amendments after they were passed. In the 1960s it wasn't Johnson and Kennedy who were the leaders and initiators of the movement for race equality, but it was black people.

In addition to focusing on social movements and having a more consciously anti-racist perspective, what are some other thematic ways in which the teaching of history must change?

I think the issue of class and class conflict needs to be addressed more honestly because it is ignored in traditional nationalist history. This is true not just of the United States but of other countries. Nationhood is a cover for extreme conflicts among classes in society, in our country, from its founding, from the making of the Constitution. Too often, there's a tendency to overlook these conflicts, and concentrate on the creation of a national identity.

Picket sign from a protest in 1941 during a time of heightened labor unrest, when Walt Disney fired union organizers on his art staff.

How does a teacher deal with the intersection of race, class, and gender in terms of U.S. history, in particular that the white working class has often been complicit, consciously or unconsciously, in some very unforgivable actions?

The complicity of poor white people in racism, the complicity of males in sexism, is a very important issue. It seems to me that complicity can't be understood without showing the intense hardships that poor white people faced in this country, making it easier for them to look for scapegoats for their condition. You have to recognize the problems of white working people in order to understand why they turn racist, because they aren't born racist.

When discussing the Civil War, teachers should point out that only a small percentage of the white population of the South owned slaves. The rest of the white population was poor and they were driven to support slavery and to be racist by the messages of those who controlled society—that they would be better off if the Negroes were put in a lower position, and that those calling for black equality were threatening the lives of these ordinary white people.

In the history of labor struggles, you should show how blacks and whites were used against one another, how white workers would go out on strike and then black people, desperate themselves for jobs, would be brought in to replace the white workers, how all-white craft unions excluded black workers, and how all this creates murderously intense racial antagonisms. So the class and race issues are very much intertwined, as is the gender issue.

One of the ways of giving some satisfaction to men who are themselves exploited is to make them masters in their own household. So they may be humiliated on the job, but they come back home and humiliate their wives and their children. There's a wonderful short story by a black woman writer, Ann Petry, "Like a Winding Sheet" that should be required reading in school. It's about a black man who is humiliated on the job and comes home and, on the flimsiest of reasons, beats his wife. The story is told in such a way as to make you really understand the pent-up anger that explodes inside a family as a result of what happens out in the world. In all these instances of racial and sexual mistreatment, it is important for students to understand that the roots of such hostility are social, environmental, situational, and are not an inevitability of human nature. It is also important to show how these antagonisms so divide people from one another as to make it difficult for them to solve their common problems in united action.

How can you teach white students to take an anti-racist perspective that isn't based merely on guilt over the things that white people have done to people of color?

If such a perspective is based only on guilt, it doesn't have a secure foundation. It has to be based on empathy and on self-interest, on an understanding that the divisions between black and white have not just resulted in the exploitation of black people, even though they've been the greatest victims, but have prevented whites and blacks from getting together to bring about the social change that would benefit them all. Showing the self-interest is also important in order to avoid the patronizing view of feeling sorry for someone, of giving somebody equality because you feel guilty about what has been done to them.

At the same time, to approach the issue merely on the basis of self-interest would be wrong, because people should learn to empathize with other people even where there is no visible, immediate self-interest.

Questions of right and wrong and justice are exactly the questions that should be raised all the time.

In response to concerns about multiculturalism, there's more lip service to include events and perspectives affecting women and people of color. But often it's presented as more facts and people to learn, without any fundamental change in perspective. What would be the approach of a truly anti-racist, multicultural perspective in U.S. history?

I've noticed this problem in some of the new textbooks, which obviously are trying to respond to the need for a multicultural approach. What I find is a bland eclecticism where everything has equal weight. You add more facts; you add more continents; you add more cultures; you add more people. But then it becomes a confusing melange in which you've added a lot of different elements but without any real emphasis on what had previously been omitted. You're left with a kind of unemotional, cold combination salad.

You need the equivalent of affirmative action in education. What affirmative action does is to say, look, things have been slanted one way for a long time. We're going to pay special attention to this person or to this group of people because they have been left out for so long.

People ask me why in my book, *A People's History of the United States*, I did not simply take the things that I put in and add them to the orthodox approaches so, as they put it, the book would be better balanced. But there's a way in which this so-called balance leaves people nowhere, with no moral sensibility, no firm convictions, no outrage, no indignation, no energy to go anywhere.

I think it is important to pay special attention to the history of black people, of Indians, of women, in a way that highlights not only the facts but the emotional intensity of such issues.

Is it possible for history to be objective?

Objectivity is neither possible nor desirable.

It's not possible because all history is subjective, all history represents a point of view. History is always a selection from an infinite number of facts and everybody makes the selection differently, based on their values and what they think is important. Since it's not possible to be objective, you should be honest about that.

Objectivity is not desirable because if we want to have an effect on the world, we need to emphasize those things which will make students more active citizens and more moral people.

How can a progressive teacher promote a radical perspective within a bureaucratic, conservative institution? Teachers sometimes either push the limits so far that they alienate their colleagues or get fired, or they're so afraid that they tone down what they really think. How can a teacher resolve this dilemma?

The problem certainly exists on the college and university level—people want to get tenure; they want to keep teaching; they want to get promoted; they want to get salary raises; and so there are all these economic punishments if they do something that looks outlandish and radical and different. But I've always believed that the main problem with college and university teachers has been self-censorship. I suspect that the same thing is true in the high schools, although you have to be more sympathetic with high school teachers because they operate in a much more repressive atmosphere. I've seen again and again where college and university teachers don't really have a problem in, for instance, using my *People's History* in their classrooms, but high school teachers always have a problem. They can't get it officially adopted; they have to get permission; they have to photocopy parts of it themselves in order to pass it out to the students; they have to worry about parents complaining, about what the head of the department or the principal or the school superintendent will say.

But I still believe, based on a lot of contact with high school teachers over the past few years, that while there's a danger of becoming overly assertive and insensitive to how others might view you, the most common behavior is timidity. Teachers withdraw and use the real fact of outside control as an excuse for teaching in the orthodox way.

Teachers need to take risks. The problem is how to minimize those risks. One important way is to make sure that you present material in class making it clear that it is subjective, that it is controversial, that you are not laying down the law for students. Another important thing is to be extremely tolerant of students who disagree with your views, or students who express racist or sexist ideas. I don't mean tolerant in the sense of not challenging such ideas, but tolerant in the sense of treating them as human beings. It's important to develop a reputation that you don't give kids poor grades on the basis of their disagreements with you. You need to create an atmosphere of freedom in the classroom.

It's also important to talk with other teachers to gain support and encouragement, to organize. Where there are teacher unions, those are logical places for teachers to support and defend one another. Where there are not teacher unions, teachers should always think how they can organize and create a collective strength.

Teachers don't always know where to get those other perspectives. Do you have any tips?

The orthodox perspective is easy to get. But once teachers begin to look for other perspectives, once they start out on that road, they will quickly be led from one thing to another to another.

So it's not as daunting as people might think?

No. It's all there. It's in the library. ■

This interview first appeared in the Rethinking Schools book, Rethinking Our Classrooms: Teaching for Equity and Justice, Vol. 1.

Discovering Columbus

Re-reading the Past

MOST OF MY STUDENTS HAVE TROUBLE with the idea that a book—especially a textbook—can lie. That's why I start my U.S. history class by stealing a student's purse.

As the year opens, my students may not know when the Civil War was fought or what James Madison or Frederick Douglass did; but they know that a brave fellow named Christopher Columbus discovered America. Indeed, this bit of historical lore may be the only knowledge class members share in common.

What students don't know is that their textbooks have, by omission or otherwise, lied to them.

Finders, Keepers

So I begin class by stealing a student's purse. I announce that the purse is mine, obviously, because look who has it. Most students are fair-minded. They saw me take the purse off the desk so they protest: "That's not yours, it's Nikki's. You took it. We saw you." I brush these objections aside and reiterate that it is, too, mine and to prove it, I'll show all the things I have inside.

I unzip the bag and remove a brush or a comb, maybe a pair of dark glasses. A tube of lipstick works best: "This is my lipstick," I say. "There, that proves it is my purse." They don't buy it and, in fact, are mildly outraged that I would pry into someone's possessions with such utter disregard for her privacy. (I've alerted the student to the demonstration before the class, but no one else knows that.)

"OK, if it's Nikki's purse, how do you know? Why are you all so positive it's not my purse?"

Different answers: "We saw you take it; that's her lipstick, we know you don't wear lipstick; there is stuff in there with her name on it." To get the point across, I even offer to help in their effort to prove Nikki's possession: "If we had a test on the contents of the purse, who would do better, Nikki or I?" "Whose labor earned the money that bought the things in the purse, mine or Nikki's?" Obvious questions, obvious answers.

I make one last try to keep Nikki's purse: "What if I said I *discovered* this purse, then would it be mine?" A little laughter is my reward, but I don't get any takers; they still think the purse is rightfully Nikki's.

"So," I ask, "Why do we say that Columbus discovered America?"

Was It Discovery?

Now they begin to see what I've been leading up to. I ask a series of questions that implicitly link Nikki's purse and the Indians' land: Were there people on the land before Columbus arrived? Who had been on the land longer, Columbus or the Indians? Who knew the land better? The students see where I'm going—it would be hard not to. "And yet," I continue, "what is the first thing that Columbus did when he arrived in the New World?" Right: he took possession of it. After all, he had discovered the place.

We talk about phrases other than "discovery" that textbooks could use to describe what Columbus did. Students start with phrases they used to describe what I did to Nikki's purse: He stole it; he took it; he ripped it off. And others: He invaded it; he conquered it.

16th-century engraving of the cruelties to the Taínos, by Theodore de Bry.

I want students to see that the word "discovery" is loaded. The word itself carries a perspective, a bias. "Discovery" represents the point of view of the supposed discoverers. It's the invaders masking their theft. And when the word gets repeated in textbooks, those textbooks become, in the phrase of one historian, "the propaganda of the winners."

To prepare students to examine textbooks critically, we begin with alternative, and rather unsentimental, explorations of Columbus's "enterprise," as he called it. The Admiral-to-be was not sailing for mere adventure and to prove the world was round, as I learned in 4th grade, but to secure the tremendous profits that were to be made by reaching the Indies.

Mostly I want the class to think about the human beings Columbus was to "discover"— and then destroy. I read from a letter Columbus wrote to Lord Raphael Sanchez, treasurer of Aragón and one of his patrons, dated March 14, 1493, following his return from the first voyage.

He reports being enormously impressed by the indigenous people:

As soon ... as they see that they are safe and have laid aside all fear, they are very simple and honest and exceedingly liberal with all they have; none of them refusing anything he may possess when he is asked for it, but, on the contrary, inviting us to ask them. They exhibit great love toward all others in preference to themselves. They also give objects of great value for trifles, and content themselves with very little or nothing in return ... I did not find, as some of us had expected, any cannibals among them, but, on the contrary, men of great deference and kindness.

But, on an ominous note, Columbus writes in his log, "should your Majesties command it, all the inhabitants could be taken away to Castile [Spain], or made slaves on the island. With 50 men we could subjugate them all and make them do whatever we want."

I ask students if they remember from elementary school days what Columbus brought back from the Americas. Students recall that he returned with parrots, plants, some gold, and a few of the people Columbus had taken to calling "Indians." This was Columbus's first expedition and it is also where most school textbook accounts of Columbus end—conveniently.

But what about his second voyage?

I read to them a passage from Hans Koning's book, *Columbus: His Enterprise*:

We are now in February 1495. Time was short for sending back a good "dividend" on the supply ships getting ready for the return to Spain. Columbus therefore turned to a massive slave raid as a means for filling up these ships. The [Columbus] brothers rounded up 1,500 Arawaks [Taínos]—men, women, and children—and imprisoned them in pens in Isabela, guarded by men and dogs. The ships had room for no more than 500, and thus only the best specimens were loaded aboard. The Admiral then told the Spaniards they could help themselves from the remainder to as many slaves as they wanted. Those whom no one chose were simply kicked out of their pens. Such had been the terror of these prisoners that (in the description by Michele de Cuneo, one of the colonists) "they rushed in all directions like lunatics, women dropping and abandoning infants in the rush, running for miles without stopping, fleeing across mountains and rivers."

Of the 500 slaves, 300 arrived alive in Spain, where they were put up for sale in Seville by Don Juan de Fonseca, the archdeacon of the town. "As naked as the day they were born," the report of this excellent churchman says, "but with no more embarrassment than animals ..."

The slave trade immediately turned out to be "unprofitable, for the slaves mostly died." Columbus decided to concentrate on gold, although he writes, "Let us in the name of the Holy Trinity go on sending all the slaves that can be sold."

Looking Through Different Eyes

Students and I role-play a scene from Columbus's second voyage. Slavery is not producing the profits Columbus is seeking. He believes there is gold and the Taíno people are selfishly holding out on him.

Students play Columbus; I play the Taínos: "Chris, we don't have any gold, honest. Can we go back to living our lives now and you can go back to wherever you came from?"

I call on several students to respond to the Taínos' plea. Columbus thinks the Taínos are lying. Student responses range from sympathetic to ruthless: OK, we'll go home; please bring us your gold; we'll lock you up in prison if you don't bring us your gold; we'll torture you if you don't fork it over, etc.

---

*"Discovery" represents
the point of view of the
supposed discoverers.
It's the invaders
masking their theft.*

After I've pleaded for a while and the students-as-Columbus have threatened, I read aloud another passage from Koning's book, describing Columbus's system for extracting gold from the Taínos:

Every man and woman, every boy or girl of fourteen or older, in the province of Cibao ... had to collect gold for the Spaniards. As their measure, the Spaniards used ... hawks' bells. ... Every three months, every [Taíno] had to bring to one of the forts a hawks' bell filled with gold dust. The chiefs had to bring in about ten times that amount. In the other provinces of Hispaniola, twenty-five pounds of spun cotton took the place of gold.

Copper tokens were manufactured, and when a [Taíno] had brought his or her tribute to an armed post, he or she received such a token, stamped with the month, to be hung around the neck. With that they were safe for another three months while collecting more gold.

Whoever was caught without a token was killed by having his or her hands cut off ... There were no gold fields, and thus, once the [Taínos] had handed in whatever they still had in gold ornaments, their only hope was to work all day in the streams, washing out gold dust from the pebbles. It was an impossible task, but those Taínos who tried to flee into the mountains were systematically hunted down with dogs and killed, to set an example for the others to keep trying. ...

During those two years of the administration of the brothers Columbus, an estimated one half of the entire population of Hispaniola was killed or killed themselves. The estimates run from one hundred and twenty-five thousand to one-half million.

The goal is not to titillate or stun, but to force the question: Why wasn't I told this before?

Columbus kneels in pious glory in a typical children's biography. This one is James de Kay's Meet Christopher Columbus.

Re-examining Basic Truths

I ask students to find a textbook, preferably one they used in elementary school, and critique the book's treatment of Columbus and the Taínos. I distribute the following handout and review the questions aloud. I don't want them to merely answer the questions, but to consider them as guidelines.

- How factually accurate was the account?

- What was omitted—left out—that in your judgment would be important for a full understanding of Columbus (for example, his treatment of the Taínos; slave-taking; his method of getting gold; the overall effect on the Taínos)?

- What motives does the book give to Columbus? Compare those with his real motives.

- Who does the book get you to root for, and how is that accomplished? (For example, are the books horrified at the treatment of Taínos or thrilled that Columbus makes it to the so-called New World?)

- How do the publishers use illustrations? What do these communicate about Columbus and his "enterprise"?

- In your opinion, why does the book portray the Columbus/Taíno encounter the way it does?

- Can you think of any groups in our society who might have an interest in people having an inaccurate view of history?

I tell students that this last question is tough but crucial. Is the continual distortion of Columbus simply an accident, or are there social groups that benefit from children developing a false or limited understanding of the past?

The assignment's subtext is to teach students that all written material should be read skeptically. I want students to explore the politics of print—that perspectives on history and social reality underlie the written word, and that to read is both to comprehend what is written, but also to question why it is written. My intention is not to encourage an "I-don't-believe-any-thing" cynicism, but rather to equip students to analyze a writer's assumptions and determine what is and isn't useful in any particular work. Reading is a metaphor. How we encourage students to approach written material reflects how we hope students will approach the world. Will they be mere consumers of text—and the world—or will they feel empowered to question, critique, and act?

"With 50 men we
could subjugate them
all and make them
do whatever we want."
— *Christopher Columbus, 1492*

For practice, we look at excerpts from a text-book, *The Story of American Freedom* (Macmillan, 1964). We read aloud and analyze several paragraphs. The arrival of Columbus and crew is especially revealing—and obnoxious. The reader watches the events from the Spaniards' point of view. We are told how Columbus and his men "fell upon their knees and gave thanks to God," a passage included in virtually all elementary school accounts of Columbus. "He then took possession of it [the island] in the name of King Ferdinand and Queen Isabella of Spain." The narrative does not question Columbus's right to assume control over a land that was already occupied. The account is so respectful of the Admiral that students can't help but sense it approves of what is, quite simply, an act of naked imperialism.

The book keeps us close to God and the Church throughout its narrative. Upon returning from the "New World"—new to whom?—Columbus shows off his parrots and "Indians." Immediately following the show, "the king and queen lead the way to a near-by church. There a song of praise and thanksgiving is sung." Intended or not, linking church and Columbus removes him still further from criticism.

Students' Conclusions

I give students a week before I ask them to bring in their written critiques. Students share their papers with one another in small groups. They note themes that recur in the papers and any differences that emerge. Here are excerpts from some students' papers in an 11th-grade literature and U.S. history class that Linda Christensen and I co-taught at Jefferson High School in Portland, Ore.

Matthew wrote: "As people read their evaluations the same situations in these textbooks came out. Things were conveniently left out so that you sided with Columbus's quest to 'boldly go where no man has gone before.' ... None of the harsh violent reality is confronted in these so-called true accounts."

Gina tried to explain why the books were so consistently rosy:

It seemed to me as if the publishers had just printed up some "glory story" that was supposed to make us feel more patriotic about our country. In our group, we talked about the possibility of the government trying to protect young students from such violence. We soon decided that that was probably one of the farthest things from their minds. They want us to look at our country as great, and powerful, and forever right. They want us to believe Columbus was a real hero. We're being fed lies. We don't question the facts, we just absorb information that is handed to us because we trust the role models that are handing it out.

Rebecca's reflected the general tone of disillusion with the textbooks: "Of course, the writers of the books probably think it's harmless enough—what does it matter who discovered America, really; and besides, it makes them feel good about America. But the thought that I have been lied to all my life about this, and who knows what else, really makes me angry."

Why Do We Do This?

The students' written reflections became the basis for a class discussion. Repeatedly, students blasted their textbooks for giving readers inadequate, and ultimately untruthful, understandings. While we didn't press to arrive at definitive explanations for the omissions and distortions, we tried to underscore the contemporary abuses of historical ignorance. If the books wax romantic about Columbus planting the flag on island beaches and taking possession of land occupied by naked red-skinned Indians, what do young readers learn from this about today's world? That might—or wealth—makes right? That it's justified to take people's land if you are more "civilized" or have a "better" religion? That white people have the right to rule over people of color?

Reading is a metaphor. How we encourage students to approach written material reflects how we hope students will approach the world.

Whatever the answers, the textbooks condition students to accept inequality; nowhere do they suggest that the Taínos were sovereign peoples with a right to control their own lands. And, if Columbus's motives are mystified or ignored, then students are less apt to question U.S. involvements in, say, Central America or the Middle East. As Bobby, approaching his registration day for the military draft, pointed out in class: "If people thought they were going off to war to fight for profits, maybe they wouldn't fight as well, or maybe they wouldn't go."

It's important to note that some students are troubled by these myth-popping discussions. One student wrote that she was "left not knowing who

to believe." Josh was the most articulate in his skepticism. He had begun to "read" our class from the same critical distance from which we hoped students would approach textbooks:

> *I still wonder ... If we can't believe what our first grade teachers told us, why should we believe you? If they lied to us, why wouldn't you? If one book is wrong, why isn't another? What is your purpose in telling us about how awful Chris was? What interest do you have in telling us the truth? What is it you want from us?*

These were wonderful questions. Linda and I responded by reading them (anonymously) to the entire class. We asked students to take a few minutes to write additional questions and comments on the Columbus activities or to imagine our response as teachers—what was the point of our lessons?

We hoped students would see that the intent was to present a new way of reading, and ultimately, of experiencing the world. Textbooks fill students with information masquerading as final truth and then ask students to parrot back the information in end-of-the-chapter "checkups." We wanted to tell students that they shouldn't necessarily trust the "authorities," but instead need to participate in their learning, probing for unstated assumptions and unasked questions.

Josh asked what our "interest" was in this approach. It's a vital question. Linda and I see teaching as political action: we want to equip students to build a truly democratic society. As Brazilian educator Paulo Freire once wrote, to be an actor for social change one must "read the word and the world."

We hope that if a student maintains a critical distance from the written word, then it's possible to maintain that same distance from one's society: to stand back, look hard, and ask, "Why is it like this? Who benefits and who suffers?"

And finally: "How can I make it better?" ▪

This article first appeared in the Rethinking Schools book Rethinking Columbus, *edited by Bill Bigelow and Bob Peterson.*

The People vs. Columbus, et al.

THIS ROLE PLAY BEGINS with the premise that a monstrous crime was committed in the years after 1492, when perhaps as many as three million or more Taínos on the island of Hispaniola lost their lives. (Most scholars estimate the number of people on Hispaniola in 1492 at between one and three million; some estimates are lower and some much higher. By 1550, very few Taínos remained alive.)

Who—and/or what—was responsible for this slaughter? This is the question students confront here.

Materials Needed:

- Some construction paper suitable for making name placards.
- Colored markers.

Time Required:

The time needed for this activity can vary considerably depending on the preparation and defenses mounted by students. Teachers should allocate at least two 50-minute periods for the role play.

Suggested Procedure:

1. In preparation for class, list the names of all the "defendants" on the board: Columbus, Columbus's men, King Ferdinand and Queen Isabella, the Taínos, and the System of Empire.

2. Tell students that each of these defendants is charged with murder—the murder of the Taíno Indians in the years following 1492. Tell them that, in groups, students will portray the defendants and that you, the teacher, will be the prosecutor.

   Explain that students' responsibility will be twofold: a) to defend themselves against the charges, and b) to explain who they think is guilty and why.

   One rule: They may plead guilty if they wish, but they cannot claim sole responsibility; they must accuse at least one other defendant. At this point, students sometimes protest that it's ridiculous to charge the Taínos for their own deaths, or they may show some confusion about the "system of empire." Tell them not to worry, that it's your job as prosecutor to explain the charges. Each group will receive a written copy of the charges against them.

3. Explain the order of the activity:

   a. In their groups, they will prepare a defense against the charges contained in the indictments. It's a good idea for students to write these up, as they will be presenting these orally and may want to read a statement.

   b. Before the trial begins, you will choose several students, who will be sworn to neutrality. These people will be the jury.

   c. As prosecutor, you will begin by arguing the guilt of a particular group.

   d. Those in the group accused by the prosecutor will then defend themselves and

will state who they believe is guilty and why. [One option is to require that each group call at least one witness. For example, in one class, the group representing the King and Queen called one of the Taínos to the stand and asked, "Have you ever seen me before?" No. "Did I ever kill any of your people?" No. "Did I ever hurt any of your people?" No. "We have no further questions."]

e. The jury will then question that group, and others may also question the group and offer rebuttals.

f. This process is repeated until all the groups have been accused and have defended themselves. The jury will then decide guilt and innocence.

4. Ask students to count off into five groups of roughly equal numbers. To get things moving quickly, I like to tell students that the first

group to circle up gets first pick of who they'll represent. Go around to each of the groups and distribute the appropriate "indictment" sheets. Remind students to read the indictment against them carefully and discuss possible arguments in their defense.

As they discuss, I wander from group to group, making sure students understand their responsibilities—at times playing devil's advocate, at times helping them consider possible defenses. Also, at this point, I distribute a placard and marker to each group so that they can display which role they are portraying.

Sometimes students want to see the indictments against the other groups. I encourage them to read these because it will help students develop additional arguments. Also, students may want to use other "evidence." [See the first chapter of Howard Zinn's *A People's History of the United States* and information included throughout the Rethinking Schools book *Rethinking Columbus*—for example, from Columbus's diary (p. 96), the timeline (p. 99), or the Taínos (p. 106).]

5. When each group appears ready—after perhaps a half hour, depending on the class—choose a jury: one member from each group (in a big class), or a total of three students in a smaller class. Publicly swear them to neutrality; they no longer represent the King and Queen, the Taínos, or anyone else.

6. The order of prosecution is up to you. I prefer: Columbus, Columbus's men, the King and Queen, the Taínos, and the System of Empire. I save the System for last as it's the most difficult to prosecute, and depends on having heard the other groups' presentations. As mentioned, the teacher argues the indictment for each group, the group defends, the jury questions, and other groups may then question. Then, the process repeats itself for each indictment. The written indictments

should be an adequate outline for prosecution, but I always feel free to embellish.

7. After each group has been charged and has made its defense, I ask the jury to step out of the classroom and deliberate. They can assign "percentage guilt," e.g., one party is 25 percent guilty, another 60 percent, etc. They also need to offer clear explanations for why they decided as they did. As they deliberate, I ask the rest of the class to step out of their roles and to do in writing the same thing the jury is doing.

8. The jury returns and explains its verdict and then we discuss. Here are some questions and issues to raise:

- Was anyone entirely not guilty? Did the prosecutor convince you that the Taínos were in part responsible for their own deaths?

- Why *didn't* the Taínos kill Columbus on his first voyage?

- How did you weigh responsibility between the "bosses" and the men they hired?

- Can you imagine a peaceful meeting between Europeans and Taínos? Or did European life—the "System of Empire"—make violence inevitable? How would Spain and other European countries have had to be different to have made a more peaceful outcome possible?

- What more would you need to know about the System of Empire to understand how it affected people's thinking and behavior?

- If the System of Empire is guilty, what should be the "sentence"? You can't put a system in prison. ■

This role play first appeared in the Rethinking Schools book Rethinking Columbus, *edited by Bill Bigelow and Bob Peterson.*

Columbus

The Indictment:

You are charged with the mistreatment and
murder of thousands, perhaps millions, of Taíno Indians.

YOUR FIRST ACT IN THE LANDS you "discovered" was to take possession of another people's territory in the name of an empire thousands of miles away.

From the very beginning of your time in the Indies you kidnapped Taíno Indians. Even when they attempted to escape, making it clear that they wanted to leave, you refused to release them.

Your journal shows that your only wish in the Indies was to find gold. The only reason you showed any kindness to the Taínos on your first trip was so they would agree to show you the source of their gold.

On your second voyage to the Indies, you ordered your men to round up Taínos and had over 500 shipped to Spain as slaves. You told your men to help themselves to the remaining Taíno captives, which they did. This act alone killed several hundred Taínos.

In 1495 you started the policy of forcing Taínos, age 14 and older, to collect gold for you. Those who didn't return every three months with the amount of gold you demanded were punished by having their hands chopped off.

You ordered your men to spread "terror" among the Taínos when there was rumor of resistance.

The list goes on. When you arrived on Hispaniola there may have been as many as a million or even three million Taínos on the island. According to one Spanish priest, by 1542 there were 200 Taínos left. There is no one to blame but you.

You were Admiral, you were Viceroy, you were Governor of the island. ■

— *from the role play,* The People vs. Columbus, et al.

Columbus's Men

The Indictment:

You are charged with the mistreatment and murder of thousands, perhaps millions, of Taíno Indians.

WITHOUT YOU, COLUMBUS'S ORDERS to enslave and kill Taínos would have been empty words.

There is no evidence that Columbus personally captured slaves or killed anyone with his own hands. You are the ones responsible for the enslavement of first hundreds, then thousands, of Taíno Indians.

You did the dirty work. You raped women. You set dogs on infants. You cut the hands off Taínos who didn't deliver enough gold. You whipped Taínos if they didn't work hard enough in the mines.

Without you there were no crimes.

You may try to blame your superiors, Columbus or even King Ferdinand and Queen Isabella. But because someone orders you to commit a crime does not free you of the blame for committing it. You could have said no. There were Spaniards, like the priests Antonio de Montesinos and Bartolomé de las Casas, who refused to mistreat Indians and spoke out on their behalf. Why didn't you?

Without the soldier there is no war.

Without you there would have been no genocide. ■

— *from the role play,* The People vs. Columbus, et al.

King Ferdinand and Queen Isabella

The Indictment:
You are charged with the mistreatment and murder of thousands, perhaps millions, of Taíno Indians.

WITHOUT YOUR MONEY, Columbus couldn't have launched his plan to find the East Indies by sailing west. Without you, he was an unemployed sailor.

You hired him to "discover" and claim new lands. Thus you are guilty of conspiracy to steal the territory of people you didn't even know, who had never bothered or harmed you.

When Columbus returned after his first voyage with several Indian captives, and you rewarded him, you became guilty of kidnapping. You could have ordered Columbus to stop kidnapping Indians. You could have punished him for this illegal act. By not doing anything to stop Columbus and his men, you legalized every crime they committed.

In his first letter to you, Columbus wrote that the Indians would make excellent slaves. Right away, you could have ordered him to take no slaves. You did no such thing, and thus became accomplices in all future slave-taking. True, after a while you discouraged Columbus from enslaving people—they mostly died, anyway—but you never punished him for these crimes, which killed hundreds of human beings.

Really, you didn't care what Columbus did, so long as you got rich. At times, you would order that the Taínos should be treated humanely. But you took no action to stop the Taínos from being forced to work in the mines. They were slaves in everything but name. Had you wanted the cruelty to stop, you could have ordered all your subjects home. But then you wouldn't have gotten any more gold. And that was what you wanted, right?

Because Columbus was unpopular with other Spaniards, you replaced him as governor. But you never punished him for the crimes committed against Taínos when he was governor. And these crimes continued under the next governor.

Because you were the bosses and because you paid the bills, you have more guilt than had you been the ones wielding the swords and hangmen's nooses. ■

— *from the role play,* The People vs. Columbus, et al.

Taínos

The Indictment:

You are charged with the mistreatment and murder of thousands, perhaps millions, of Taíno Indians.

WHILE YOU ARE THE VICTIMS of this crime, you are also guilty of committing it. You failed to fight back against the Spaniards. This meant that you brought the fate of slavery and death upon yourselves.

From the very beginning you must have known what Columbus meant to do. He took Taíno captives from other islands and held them against their will. He claimed your land as his own. He was interested only in finding gold. When your people were cut by Spaniards' swords, Columbus and his men showed no concern. All this you must have known.

Tragically, you let this greedy, violent man get away, so he could return. On his next trip, however, he brought 17 ships and between 1,200 and 1,500 men, all heavily armed. You allowed, even invited, this invasion.

Foolishly, your *cacique* (leader), Caonabó, killed the 39 men Columbus left behind. Why didn't Caonabó and the Taínos kill all the Spaniards—including Columbus—before they had a chance to return to Spain? Imagine the different outcome had the Taínos been smart enough to stop Columbus before he could launch the invasion.

Who knows why the Taínos of Hispaniola did not unite to throw out all the

Spaniards? Had Taínos worked together they might have beaten the Spaniards even after Columbus returned. After all, the Spaniards numbered fewer than 2,000; Taínos numbered in the hundreds of thousands, possibly as many as three million.

However, as a result of this Taíno failure, all the Native peoples of the Americas suffered. ◼

— *from the role play,* The People vs. Columbus, et al.

The System of Empire

The Indictment:
You are charged with the mistreatment and
murder of thousands, perhaps millions, of Taíno Indians.

THIS GETS COMPLICATED. You are not a person, but a system. We like to blame crimes on people. But in this case, the real criminal is not human.

True, Columbus's men did the killing, Columbus gave the orders and King Ferdinand and Queen Isabella paid the bills—and took the profits. But what made them behave the way they did? Were they born evil and greedy? The real blame lies with a system that values property over people.

European society was organized so that an individual had to own property to feel secure. The more property one owned, the more security, the more control over one's destiny. There was no security without private ownership of property. If you were poor, you could starve. The Taínos were not perfect, but they had no "poor" and no one starved. Indians commented that Europeans' love of gold was like a disease. In fact, this attitude was a product of a diseased system.

In order to get more wealth, Columbus and his men took Taínos as slaves, terrorized them into searching out gold and forced them to work on their farms and in their mines. They justified all this by telling themselves that the Taínos weren't Christian, so "we" can control "their" land and labor. The European system saw only white Christians as full human beings.

It was life in a system that valued private property (especially gold), and approved of violence against foreigners and non-Christians to get it, that made Columbus and his men enslave and kill. Sane people do not kill hundreds of thousands of other human beings. It was a rotten, insane system that led Columbus and the others to behave the way they did. You, as the representatives of this system, are guilty for the genocide committed against Taínos.

As a final test to see who is guilty for the mass murder of the Taínos, ask yourself these questions:

- If it had been some other "explorer" besides Columbus to "discover America," would he have let the Taínos keep their land?

- Would he not have enslaved people?

- Would he not have made them search for gold and work in the mines?

You know the answer: Any European conqueror would have been every bit as bad as Columbus. Why? Because the system of empire was to blame, not any particular individual. ■

— from the role play, The People vs. Columbus, et al.

U.S.–Mexico War Tea Party:

"We Take Nothing by Conquest, Thank God"

TODAY'S BORDER WITH MEXICO is the product of invasion and war. Grasping some of the motives for that war and some of its immediate effects begins to provide students the kind of historical context that is crucial for thinking intelligently about the line that separates the United States and Mexico. The tea party activity introduces students to a number of the individuals and themes they will encounter in Howard Zinn's "We Take Nothing by Conquest, Thank God."

Materials Needed:

- Tea party roles, cut up. One for every student in the class.
- Blank nametags. Enough for every student in the class.
- Copies of "The War with Mexico: Questions" for every student.
- Copies of "We Take Nothing by Conquest, Thank God" for every student.
- Copies of U.S.-Mexico map, p. 48.
- Copies of the student handout, "The War with Mexico."

Time Required:

- One class period for the tea party. Time for follow-up discussion.
- A portion of one class period to assign "We Take Nothing by Conquest, Thank God," and a portion of another to discuss.
- A portion of one class period to read and critique "The War with Mexico" textbook excerpt.

Suggested Procedure:

1. Explain to students that they are going to do an activity about the U.S. war with Mexico, 1846-1848. Distribute one tea party role to each student in the class. There are only 21, so in most classes, some students will be assigned the same historical character. (Most but not all of the roles are based on individuals included in Zinn's "We Take Nothing by Conquest, Thank God," as the tea party is intended as a pre-reading activity. A couple are drawn from the chapter, "Foreigners in Their Own Land: Manifest Destiny in the Southwest," in Ronald Takaki's *A Different Mirror*; others are based on material in Milton Meltzer's *Bound for the Rio Grande*, Matt S. Meier and Feliciano Rivera's *The Chicanos: A History of Mexican Americans*, Elizabeth Martínez's *500 Años del Pueblo Chicano/500 Years of Chicano History in Pictures*, and Deena J. González's "The Widowed Women of Santa Fe: Assessments on the Lives of an Unmarried Population, 1850-1880" in *Unequal Sisters: A Multicultural Reader in U.S. Women's History*, Ellen Carol DuBois and Vicki L. Ruiz, eds.)

2. Have students fill out their nametags, using the name of the individual they are assigned. Tell students that in this activity you would like each of them to attempt to become these people from history. Ask students to read their roles several times and to memorize as much of the information as possible. Encourage them to underline key points. Sometimes it helps if students turn over their roles and list three or four facts about their characters that they think are most important.

3. Distribute a copy of "The War with Mexico: Questions" to every student. Explain their assignment: Students should circulate through the classroom, meeting other individuals from the U.S.-Mexico War. They should use the questions on the sheet as a guide to talk with others about the war and to complete the questions as fully as possible. They must use a different individual to answer each of the eight questions. (This is not the *Twilight Zone*, so students who have been assigned the same person may not meet themselves.) Tell them that it's not a race; the aim is for students to spend time hearing each other's stories, not just hurriedly scribbling down answers to the different questions. I like to begin this activity by asking for a student volunteer to demonstrate with me an encounter between two of the individuals, so that the rest of the class can sense the kind of interaction I'm looking for.

4. Ask students to stand up and begin to circulate throughout the class to meet one another and to fill out responses on the U.S.-Mexico War questions student handout.

5. Afterwards, ask students to share some of their findings with the whole class. This needn't be exhaustive, as students will learn a lot more about these issues when they read the excerpt from Howard Zinn's *A People's History of the United States*. Possible questions:

   • What surprised you about this activity?

   • Who found someone with opinions different than your character's opinions?

• What were some of the different points of view you found on why the United States and Mexico went to war?

• Why do you think the United States and Mexico went to war?

• What were some results of the war?

• What questions does this activity leave you with?

"We Take Nothing by Conquest, Thank God"

6. As follow-up, assign Howard Zinn's "We Take Nothing by Conquest, Thank God" and the U.S.-Mexico map (see p. 48). Another reading to consider using is Milton Meltzer's chapter focusing on the U.S. soldiers from Ireland who went over to the Mexican side as the San Patricio Battalion, "Traitors—or Martyrs," from his book *Bound for the Rio Grande*. Similarly, I've used the song, "San Patricio Brigade," included on *New York Town*, a CD by the Irish-American rock group Black 47 to talk with students about the Irish resistance to the war. Black 47 can at first-listen sound odd, but my students seemed to enjoy hearing this raucous song about a "boy from the green fields of Galway." A poignant song/powerpoint is David Rovics' "Saint Patrick's Battalion," posted on YouTube.

7. Ask students to complete a "talk-back" journal with the Zinn reading. They should locate at least five passages from the reading that they found amusing, important, startling, moving, confusing, outrageous, or odd. They should write out each quote and their detailed reaction to it. You might ask students to find material that they can connect with information they learned in the tea party, events that relate somehow to their own lives or things going on today. Also encourage students to raise at least two questions that they would like to discuss with the rest of the class.

8. In addition to students' own questions, here are some questions for further discussion or writing:

- Why did the United States government want to obtain California?

- What is meant by the term Manifest Destiny?

- What were the pressures on the United States government to push for expansion?

- What if you believed the war with Mexico was immoral, but both major parties, Democratic and Whig, supported it? What would you do to try to bring an end to the war?

- Re-read Abraham Lincoln's quote on p. 41. Lincoln believes that even though Whigs opposed the war before it began, that once the war began they should allocate money to support the war. Explain why you agree or disagree.

- Comment on the belief of some Americans: The Mexican War was a good thing, because it gave the blessings of liberty and democracy to more people.

- In what ways could it be said that the Mexican War was a racist war? Give examples.

- Describe the resistance to the war. How effective was the opposition?

- From a Mexican standpoint, given the origins and nature of the U.S.-Mexico War, how might people today respond to the efforts to exclude Mexicans from U.S. territory, and treat them as criminals once they are here?

- In his essay "On Civil Disobedience," Henry David Thoreau writes that what is *legal* is not necessarily what is *right*. Do you agree? Can you think of any examples from history or current events?

- The Reverend Theodore Parker said that Mexicans must eventually give way, as did the Indians. What similarities do you see between the Mexican War and the wars against the Indians?

- Why might ordinary citizens—workers or farmers, with no slaves and no plans to move onto Mexican territory—support the U.S. war against Mexico? Does war itself hold attraction for people, or was it the Mexican War in particular that excited some Americans?

- As was the case with the organized opposition to Indian Removal in the 1820s and 1830s, racism infected the movement against the war with Mexico. Give some examples. Why do you think this racism existed?

- If the U.S. Army was supposed to bring liberty and civilization to Mexico, why do you think rape and mistreatment of Mexicans was so widespread?

- Who benefited from the Mexican War?

Textbook Critique

Textbooks may have useful background information, photos, maps, and graphs. But often they contain biases and omissions. This activity asks students to question how one major U.S. history textbook covers the U.S. war with Mexico.

1. Distribute to students the selection from Glencoe McGraw-Hill's *American Odyssey*, a high school text, p. 49. Although the main focus of this 1,010-page textbook is the 20th century, the book includes 249 pre-20th century pages. Note that this two-paragraph section is the book's entire discussion of the U.S.-Mexico War. (As an alternative to using the excerpt provided, you might ask students to use their own textbooks, or distribute several different texts so they can compare coverage.)

2. Ask students to read the textbook excerpt individually and to consider the accompanying questions. Encourage them to use these questions as a guide, but tell them that you're interested in whatever insights they generate. Also encourage students to write comments and questions on the excerpt itself—to "talk back" to the textbook. I find

that when students begin marking up a passage it can have an empowering effect; it affirms their right to have an opinion that differs from that of the "authority." And they realize that they know important things that a text may have omitted or distorted.

3. Ask students to turn to one or two students around them and share their thoughts about the reading.

4. Bring students back together to discuss. Some questions in addition to the two on the handout:

- If everything that students knew about the U.S. war with Mexico came from this textbook, do you suppose they'd think the war was right or wrong? Explain.

- How does this account differ from what they learned in the tea party and in Howard Zinn's account in "We Take Nothing by Conquest, Thank God"?

- In the textbook excerpt, what do you learn about the *causes* of the war with Mexico? What *doesn't* the book tell you about the causes?

- What does the textbook tell about the many American citizens who opposed U.S. involvement in the war? What difference does it make when textbooks fail to tell students about individuals and movements in history that opposed government policies?

- What does the textbook include about the experiences or activities of African Americans, Mexicans, Native Americans, or women?

- Why do you think this textbook leaves out important information?

- In the Glencoe McGraw-Hill text, the entire section on the U.S.-Mexico War consists of two paragraphs. What message might that send to readers?

5. You might allow students to act on what they find. They could write letters to a textbook company or a school district textbook selection committee, rewrite sections of the text or write critiques to be left in the book for the following year's students, and/or lead workshops with other students and young children about the omissions they uncovered.

Some Additional Activities and Projects:

- Design a monument or memorial exhibit to commemorate the U.S. war with Mexico. Consider what symbols might best represent this war. Given that your audience is likely to know little about the war, what essential points should you teach? Perhaps design the commemoration from a Mexican standpoint.

- Read Henry David Thoreau's "On Civil Disobedience" and write a response.

- Write a diary entry or letter explaining why you are volunteering to fight in Mexico. Or write a diary or letter explaining why you oppose the war and will refuse to fight.

- Write an interior monologue from the point of view of an individual mentioned in the reading or tea party—for example, a California Indian listening to naval officer Revere; a Mexican woman in Santa Fe, as General Kearny's troops enter; a volunteer U.S. soldier who is experiencing the horrors of war for the first time; one of General Cushing's men as he speaks to them at their reception dinner in Massachusetts. ■

This activity first appeared in the Rethinking Schools book The Line Between Us: Teaching About the Border and Mexican Immigration, *by Bill Bigelow.*

The War with Mexico: Roles

Colonel Ethan Allen Hitchcock

I am a professional soldier, graduate of the U.S. Military Academy, commander of the 3rd Infantry Regiment. I am an aide to General Zachary Taylor. Like President Polk, Taylor wanted a war with Mexico, and so he moved troops to the Rio Grande—territory claimed by both Mexico and Texas—to provoke the Mexicans. Eventually, the Mexicans did attack, as Taylor and Polk knew they would. And now U.S. leaders have their war. The United States doesn't have any right whatsoever to move into Mexico. The government is looking for war so that it can take over as much of Mexico as it wants. The United States is the aggressor. My heart is not in this war. But I am an officer in the U.S. Army and I must carry out my orders.

Congressman Abraham Lincoln, Whig Party, Illinois

The Whigs were accused of being opposed to the war against Mexico. Well, that's true or false, depending on how you look at it. It's true that we spoke out in Congress against the war. In a speech, I challenged President Polk to name the exact spot where Mexicans supposedly shed American blood. I was against Polk pushing this war with Mexico. But once the war started, we consistently voted to supply funds to wage the war and support the troops. In fact, I even gave a speech in Congress supporting the candidacy of General Zachary Taylor for president. And Taylor was the first general in charge of waging the war.

President James K. Polk

I won the presidency by a close vote in 1844 and now I am president of the United States of America. I am a Democrat, and a believer in "Manifest Destiny." It is God's plan that the United States should spread from the Atlantic to the Pacific. In 1846, I ordered U.S. troops into an area that was claimed both by Texas and Mexico, historically occupied by Mexicans. I knew that it was a provocation. As I confided to my Secretary of the Navy: I want California to be part of the United States. It's part of Mexico and the only way to get it away from them is war. As I'd expected, the Mexicans attacked and I convinced Congress to declare war against Mexico. Some of my opponents say that I want this war only because I own slaves and this is a war to extend slavery to Mexico. Nonsense. There is much more at stake than slavery. This is about defending America's honor and our national interest.

William Lloyd Garrison, Founder, American Anti-Slavery Society

I oppose the Mexican War, as do all true opponents of slavery. President Polk is a slave owner and like all slave owners, he wants to expand slavery everywhere. That's why this war is being fought: to steal more territory from Mexico so that Mexico can be carved up into new slave states. Mexico abolished slavery in 1829, and the Texans left Mexico and established their own "country" so that they could keep their slaves. Now Texas is entering the United States as a slave state. My organization and I will speak out, organize protest meetings, write articles, publish pamphlets, and do everything legal we can do to oppose this immoral war. In our newspaper, *The Liberator,* we have written that we hope the Mexicans will win this war. It's not a popular statement these days, but when it comes to justice, we cannot compromise.

Henry David Thoreau

I live in Concord, Massachusetts, where I work as a writer. In order to support this war with Mexico, Massachusetts passed a poll tax. I won't pay it. Simple as that. The government wants to force people into this unjust war to go kill Mexicans or be killed. I won't support that. For my "crime," they put me in jail for a night. My friend, the famous writer Ralph Waldo Emerson, came to visit me in jail. He said, "What are you doing in there?" I replied, "What are you doing out there?" Against my wishes, friends of mine paid my tax and I was released. But I have come to believe that the way to stop injustice is not merely to speak out against it, but also to refuse to obey unjust laws.

Reverend Theodore Parker

I am a Unitarian minister in Boston, Massachusetts, with a congregation of 7,000. I oppose this war with Mexico because this is a war to expand slavery. Slavery should be ended not expanded. I am not opposed to the war because I like the Mexicans. As I have written, they are "a wretched people; wretched in their origin, history and character." We Americans are vastly superior, but we must not take them over by force. We should resist this war. I urge young men not to enlist, bankers should refuse to lend money for the war, ship owners should refuse to let their ships be used for the war; manufacturers should refuse to produce cannons, swords, and gunpowder for the war. Let the government prosecute me as a traitor. I answer only to God.

María Josefa Martínez, Santa Fe, New Mexico

Two years ago, in 1846, the United States invaded Mexico. That summer, Colonel Stephen W. Kearny of the United States Army marched into Santa Fe to take control. Up until that moment, I was a Mexican woman. Since then, I have been a conquered Mexican woman. There are about 25,000 to 30,000 women in New Mexico. The white male conquerors treat us badly. They have contempt for all Mexicans, especially women. As a woman, under Mexican law I was allowed to own property in my maiden name, and sell or give it away without my husband's signature. I could even farm my own land apart from my husband's land or land that we owned together. U.S. women don't have these rights. Unlike the invaders, I speak Spanish not English. But English is the language used by lawyers, judges, and tax assessors. I worry that the U.S. authorities will use my lack of English to take away my rights and property.

Sgt. John Riley, San Patricio Battalion, Formerly U.S. Army

Originally, I'm from a small town in Ireland. I joined the U.S. Army and became a drillmaster at West Point, training men to be soldiers. Now the Army considers me a deserter and a traitor. That's not how I see it. I was sent to invade Mexico with the Army. The U.S. had no right to be there. It was like the British occupying Ireland. Mexicans were treated cruelly. The Mexicans appealed to me to leave the U.S. Army and to join theirs. And I did. I became a lieutenant and about 260 U.S. soldiers joined me fighting on the Mexican side. In Boston and Philadelphia, the Protestants had burned our Catholic churches. The Mexicans are Catholic too. But now, we are captured. Most of us have been sentenced to death by hanging. The "lucky" ones are to be given 50 lashes with a whip, forced to dig the graves for our friends who will be executed, and then branded on our cheeks with the letter "D" for deserter.

Frederick Douglass

I was born a slave. When I was about 20 years old, I ran away from my so-called master, and came to live in the north, where I have become famous speaking and writing against slavery. I publish an anti-slavery journal called the *North Star*. This war with Mexico is disgraceful and cruel. Mexico is a victim of those white people of America who love to push around people who aren't white. Unfortunately, even many abolitionists (people who are working to end slavery) have continued to pay their taxes and do not to resist this war with enough passion. It's time that we risk everything for peace.

U.S. Naval Officer

I'm a lucky man. I got to sail into California to seize that territory for the United States of America. It's ours now, not the Mexicans'. Here's what I wrote in my diary when I sailed up from South America and landed in Monterey, California: "Asia will be brought to our very doors. Population will flow into the fertile regions of California. The resources of the entire country will be developed. The public lands lying along the route of railroads will be changed from deserts into gardens, and a large population will be settled." This is where I'm going to settle after we defeat the Mexicans once and for all.

General Stephen Kearny

I command the United States Army in the West. I had the honor of winning New Mexico for the United States during the war with Mexico. The high point for me was taking the city of Santa Fe. I wanted to conquer but not to kill. I sent word that if the people didn't fight us we wouldn't fight them. We marched into Santa Fe with our bayonets and knives out, hoping that we would frighten the residents, so they would not fight us. And they didn't. We raised the American flag and fired our cannon in a glorious salute to the United States of America. Apparently this had a strong effect on the town's women because many of them let loose a "wail of grief," as one of my officers described it. The sound of their crying rose above the noise of our horses as we rode along.

U.S. Army Officer

I thought the war was going to be a lot of fun. How could the Mexicans put up much of a fight when they were up against the powerful United States? But soon enough the reality of war set in. As we moved up the Rio Grande, it was incredibly hot, hotter than I'd ever experienced. The water was bad and many of my men got diarrhea, dysentery, and other diseases. It was awful. We lost a thousand men just from sickness. I watched some men do horrible things. As I wrote in my diary: "We reached Burrita about 5 p.m., many of the Louisiana volunteers were there, a lawless drunken rabble. They had driven away the inhabitants, taken possession of their houses, and were emulating [copying] each other in making beasts of themselves." They raped many women there.

Oregon Trail, Wagon Train Member

In 1844, I took a wagon train from Missouri to the Oregon territory, but someone said there was better farmland in California, and warmer weather. So I headed south to the San Joaquin Valley. It's a part of Mexico, but there are more and more people arriving all the time from the United States. And now war has broken out. Soon this won't be Mexico anymore. It will be the United States of America. Manifest Destiny is what they call it, and from sea to shining sea, soon it will be filled with free, white, English-speaking farmers and ranchers. Too bad it's going to take a war to make it happen, but the Mexicans wouldn't sell California, and then they attacked us. So fair's fair.

Cochise, Chiricahua Apache leader

Some of the whites think that my land belongs to the United States. Some think it belongs to Mexico. They are all wrong. My land belongs to my people, the Apaches. We roam the lands that Mexico calls Sonora and that the United States considers New Mexico and Arizona. First, Spain claimed this land, then the Mexicans, now the Americans. Over the years, we've fought them all—the European invaders—and we will continue to fight. Before this latest war, the Mexicans paid Americans to help track us down. In fact, a group of them killed my father. When I was young I walked all over this country, east and west, and saw no other people than the Apaches. Now the invaders are everywhere. Mexicans, Americans: I want them all gone from my land.

Jefferson Davis, Mississippi

I'm one of the largest plantation owners in the United States. Every year, it seems that the people against slavery just get louder and louder. They're trying to keep slavery out of the Western territories like Kansas and Nebraska. And now, like a gift from God, along comes this war against Mexico. Think of all the new territory we can conquer for freedom—the freedom to take our slaves wherever we like. First Mexico, then Cuba, and then Nicaragua. I can see the day when the United States could rule all of Mexico and Central America, and all that territory will be added to our country—new states, new slave states. This is a great war. Thank heavens the Mexicans attacked us first. Justice is on our side.

General Mariano Vallejo

I live in California, a part of Mexico. I am a wealthy man. I own 175,000 acres. This is where my 16 children were born. I have always been very kind to visitors who come from the United States, and some even say that I am famous for the hospitality I show my guests. In the 1840s, more and more people from the United States began arriving. Unbelievably, most of them looked down on Mexicans, and called us "greasers," and an inferior race—we who were born here and built wealthy *ranchos*. Now that war has broken out, it is clear what the North Americans are looking for: They want to steal California away from Mexico and make it a part of the United States. Before the war, they wanted to buy California from Mexico, but Mexico wouldn't sell. So now they are making war on us so that they can take it away. I fear that I will lose everything I've worked so hard for.

Doña Francesca Vallejo

I live in California, a part of Mexico. I am a wealthy woman, a wealthy *Mexican* woman. With my husband, I own 175,000 acres. I have numerous servants. I have two for my own personal service. Four or five servants grind corn for tortillas, for we entertain so many guests that three servants could not feed them all. About six or seven work in the kitchen. Five or six are continually occupied washing the clothes of my 16 children and the rest are employed in the house; and finally, nearly a dozen attend to the sewing and spinning. This is where my children were born. I have always been very friendly to visitors who come from the United States, and some even say that I am famous for the hospitality I show my guests. And now there is a war. The United States will try to take California away from Mexico, but they have no right, and we won't let them.

Lieutenant, U.S. Army Infantry

In a place called Huamantla, the Mexicans killed one of our officers, a man by the name of Walker. He was a friend of General Lane. The general told us to "avenge the death of the gallant Walker, to take all we could lay hands on." And we did. We broke open liquor stores and got drunk. Then we went after the women and girls. They were stripped of their clothing and terrible outrages were committed against them. We shot dozens of men and ransacked their churches, stores and houses. We even killed the Mexicans' horses. Drunken U.S. soldiers were everywhere, yelling, screeching, breaking open houses or chasing Mexicans who ran for their lives. As I wrote my parents, "Such a scene I never hope to see again. It made me for the first time ashamed of my country."

Francisco Márquez, Mexican Cadet

I am a cadet, studying at a military school in Mexico City. The school is in a castle high up on a hill in the beautiful Chapultepec region of the city. I love my country and I want to defend it from the invading U.S. Army. Why are they attacking my country? Because they want to bring back slavery to Mexico? Because they want to steal California and other territories of Mexico? Why? They have done brutal things to my people. I will fight to the death. We have been ordered by our officers to leave the military school because we are too young to fight as soldiers. But I will stay and fight. I will fight until I am the last one alive, and then I will wrap myself in the Mexican flag and jump to my death before allowing myself to be captured by the Americans.

Padre Antonio José Martínez

In the struggle between the rich and the poor, I stand with the poor. In fact, I am called the Padre (Father) of the Poor. I founded the first school for boys and girls in the entire Southwest and also began one of the first newspapers in the region. And I opposed the U.S. invaders when recently they came to take over our territory in New Mexico. Even though I am a priest, many believe that I was a leader of the Revolt of Taos in 1847. On January 19, 1847, 2,000 Indians and *Mexicanos* together rose up and killed the U.S.-installed governor in his mansion as well as other U.S. officials who were stealing our land. The rebels marched through the snow and took refuge in a Catholic church in the Taos pueblo, thinking they would be safe. They weren't. The U.S. Army destroyed the church with cannon fire. The U.S. authorities put six leaders on trial and found them guilty in 15 minutes. The six men were hanged, holding hands as they died.

Wotoki, Miwok Indian, California

I live in northern California, in Sonoma. No matter who wins this war between Mexico and the United States, nothing changes the fact that this is *Miwok* land—*our* land—that they are fighting over. First, the Spaniards took over, then the Mexicans. Now the Americans are taking over. But they all mistreated the Miwok people. Our land is now owned by one of the richest men in California, the Mexican General Mariano Vallejo. They say he and his wife, Doña Francesca, are kind to visitors. But he is not kind to his Indian workers. I work on his land. Vallejo treats us almost like slaves. And the Americans here are no better. An American named Captain Sutter orders "his" Indians to eat out of four-feet-long troughs, as if Indians are pigs. Sutter whips them when they disobey. I have no idea what this war between Mexico and the United States is about. To me, it looks like Americans and Mexicans killing each other so that they can steal our land.

The War with Mexico: Questions

1. Find someone who fought in the war—on either side. Who is the person? What was their experience like?

2. Find someone who supports the U.S. war with Mexico. Who is the person? Why do they support the war?

3. Find someone who opposes the U.S. war with Mexico. Who is the person? Why do they oppose the war?

4. Find someone who has an opinion on why the United States is at war with Mexico. Who is the person? What is their opinion about why the United States is at war?

5. Find someone who saw things in the war that shocked them. Who is the person? What shocked them?

6. Find someone who lives in a different part of the country than you do—or lives in another country. Who is the person? What do you agree on about the war? What do you disagree on?

7. Find someone who stands to gain from the war. Who are they? How might they benefit?

8. Find someone who stands to lose from the war. Who are they? How might they suffer?

We Take Nothing by Conquest, Thank God

By Howard Zinn

COL. ETHAN ALLEN HITCHCOCK, a professional soldier, graduate of the Military Academy, commander of the 3rd Infantry Regiment, a reader of Shakespeare, Chaucer, Hegel, Spinoza, wrote in his diary:

> Fort Jesup, La., June 30, 1845. Orders came last evening by express from Washington City directing General Taylor to move without any delay to … take up a position on the banks of or near the Rio Grande, and he is to expel any armed force of Mexicans who may cross that river. Bliss read the orders to me last evening hastily at tattoo. I have scarcely slept a wink, thinking of the needful preparations. … Violence leads to violence, and if this movement of ours does not lead to others and to bloodshed, I am much mistaken.

Hitchcock was not mistaken. Jefferson's Louisiana Purchase had doubled the territory of the United States, extending it to the Rocky Mountains. To the southwest was Mexico, which had won its independence in a revolutionary war against Spain in 1821. Mexico was then an even larger country than it is now, since it included what are now Texas, New Mexico, Utah, Nevada, Arizona, California, and part of Colorado. After agitation, and aid from the United States, Texas broke off from Mexico in 1836 and declared itself the "Lone Star Republic." In 1845, the U.S. Congress brought it into the Union as a state.

In the White House now was James Polk, a Democrat, an expansionist, who, on the night of his inauguration, confided to his secretary of the Navy that one of his main objectives was the acquisition of California. His order to General Taylor to move troops to the Rio Grande was a challenge to the Mexicans. It was not at all clear that the Rio Grande was the southern boundary of Texas, although Texas had forced the defeated Mexican general Santa Anna to say so when he was a prisoner. The traditional border between Texas and Mexico had been the Nueces River, about 150 miles to the north, and both Mexico and the United States had recognized that as the border. However, Polk, encouraging the Texans to accept annexation, had assured them he would uphold their claims to the Rio Grande.

Ordering troops to the Rio Grande, into territory inhabited by Mexicans, was clearly a provocation. Taylor's army marched in parallel columns across the open prairie, scouts far ahead and on the flanks, a train of supplies following. Then, along a narrow road, through a belt of thick chaparral, they arrived, March 28, 1846, in cultivated fields and thatched-roof huts hurriedly abandoned by the Mexican occupants, who had fled across the river to the city of Matamoros. Taylor set up camp, began construction of

Col. Ethan Allen Hitchcock

Getty Images/Hulton Archive

a fort, and implanted his cannons facing the white houses of Matamoros, whose inhabitants stared curiously at the sight of an army on the banks of a quiet river.

'Our Manifest Destiny'

The *Washington Union*, a newspaper expressing the position of President Polk and the Democratic party, had spoken early in 1845 on the meaning of Texas annexation: "Let the great measure of annexation be accomplished, and with it the questions of boundary and claims. For who can arrest the torrent that will pour onward to the West? The road to California will be open to us. Who will stay the march of our western people?"

It was shortly after that, in the summer of 1845, that John O'Sullivan, editor of the *Democratic Review*, used the phrase that became famous, saying it was "Our manifest destiny to overspread the continent allotted by Providence for the free development of our yearly multiplying millions." Yes, manifest destiny.

All that was needed in the spring of 1846 was a military incident to begin the war that Polk wanted. It came in April, when General Taylor's quartermaster, Colonel Cross, while riding up the Rio Grande, disappeared. His body was found eleven days later, his skull smashed by a heavy blow. It was assumed he had been killed by Mexican guerrillas crossing the river.

> *"It is our manifest destiny to overspread the continent allotted by Providence for the free development of our yearly multiplying millions."*

The next day (April 25), a patrol of Taylor's soldiers was surrounded and attacked by Mexicans, and wiped out: sixteen dead, others wounded, the rest captured. Taylor sent a dispatch to Polk: "Hostilities may now be considered as commenced."

The Mexicans had fired the first shot. But they had done what the American government wanted, according to Colonel Hitchcock, who wrote in his diary, even before those first incidents:

I have said from the first that the United States are the aggressors. ... We have not one particle of right to be here. ... It looks as if the government sent a small force on purpose to bring on a war, so as to have a pretext for taking California and as much of this country as it chooses. ... My heart is not in this business ... but, as a military man, I am bound to execute orders.

On May 9, before news of any battles, Polk was suggesting to his cabinet a declaration of war. Polk recorded in his diary what he said to the cabinet meeting:

I stated ... that up to this time, as we knew, we had heard of no open act of aggression by the Mexican army, but that the danger was imminent that such acts would be committed. I said that in my opinion we had ample cause of war, and that it was impossible ... that I could remain silent much longer ... that the country was excited and impatient on the subject. ...

The country was not "excited and impatient." But the president was. When the dispatches arrived from General Taylor telling of casualties from the Mexican attack, Polk summoned the cabinet to hear the news, and they unanimously agreed he should ask for a declaration of war. Polk's message to Congress was indignant: "Mexico has passed the boundary of the United States, has invaded our territory and shed American blood upon the American soil. ..."

Congress then rushed to approve the war message. The bundles of official documents accompanying the war message, supposed to be evidence for Polk's statement, were not examined, but were tabled immediately by the House. Debate on the bill providing volunteers and money for the war was limited to two hours, and most of this was used up reading selected portions of the tabled documents, so that barely half an hour was left for discussion of the issues.

The Whig party also wanted California, but preferred to do it without war. Nevertheless, they would not deny men and money for the operation and so joined Democrats in voting overwhelmingly for the war resolution, 174 to 14. In the Senate there was debate, but it was limited to one day, and the war measure passed, 40 to 2, Whigs joining Democrats. John Quincy Adams of Massachusetts, who originally voted with "the stubborn 14," later voted for war appropriations.

Abraham Lincoln of Illinois was not yet in Congress when the war began, but after his election in 1846 he had occasion to vote and speak on the war. His "spot resolutions" became famous—he challenged Polk to specify the exact spot where American blood was shed "on the American soil." But he would not try to end the war by stopping funds for men and supplies. Speaking in the House on July 27, 1848, he said:

> *"I have said from the first that the United States are the aggressors … It looks as if the government sent a small force on purpose to bring on a war, so as to have a pretext for taking California and as much of this country as it chooses."*

> If to say "the war was unnecessarily and unconstitutionally commenced by the President" be opposing the war, then the Whigs have very generally opposed it. … The marching an army into the midst of a peaceful Mexican settlement, frightening the inhabitants away, leaving their growing crops and other property to destruction, to you may appear a perfectly amiable, peaceful, unprovoking procedure; but it does not appear so to us. … But if, when the war had begun, and had become the cause of the country, the giving of our money and our blood, in common with yours, was support of the war, then it is not true that we have always opposed the war. With few individual exceptions, you have constantly had our votes here for all the necessary supplies. …

A handful of antislavery Congressmen voted against all war measures, seeing the Mexican campaign as a means of extending the southern slave territory. One of these was Joshua Giddings of Ohio, a fiery speaker, physically powerful, who called it "an aggressive, unholy, and unjust war."

After Congress acted in May of 1846, there were rallies and demonstrations for the war in New York, Baltimore, Indianapolis, Philadelphia, and many other places. Thousands rushed to volunteer for the army. The poet Walt Whitman wrote in the *Brooklyn Eagle* in the early days of the war: "Yes: Mexico must be thoroughly chastised! … Let our arms now be carried with a spirit which shall teach the world that, while we are not forward for a quarrel, America knows how to crush, as well as how to expand!"

Accompanying all this aggressiveness was the idea that the United States would be giving the blessings of liberty and democracy to more people. This was intermingled with ideas of racial superiority, longings for the beautiful lands of New Mexico and California, and thoughts of commercial enterprise across the Pacific. *The New York Herald* said, in 1847: "The universal Yankee nation can regenerate and disenthrall the people of Mexico in a few years; and we believe it is part of our destiny to civilize that beautiful country."

The *Congressional Globe* of February 11, 1847, reported:

> Mr. Giles, of Maryland—I take it for granted, that we shall gain territory, and must gain territory, before we shut the gates of the temple of Janus. …We must march from ocean to ocean. … We must march from Texas straight to the Pacific ocean, and be bounded only by its roaring wave. … It is the destiny of the white race, it is the destiny of the Anglo-Saxon race. …

Presidential candidate Gen. Zachary Taylor sits atop a mound of skulls in this 1848 cartoon criticizing his role in the U.S. war against Mexico.

Anti-War Sentiment

The American Anti-Slavery Society, on the other hand, said the war was "waged solely for the detestable and horrible purpose of extending and perpetuating American slavery throughout the vast territory of Mexico." A 27-year-old Boston poet and abolitionist, James Russell Lowell, began writing satirical poems in the *Boston Courier* (they were later collected as the *Biglow Papers*). In them, a New England farmer, Hosea Biglow, spoke, in his own dialect, on the war:

> *Ez fer war, I call it murder —*
> *— There you hev it plain an' flat;*
> *I don't want to go no furder*
> *— Than my Testyment fer that. …*
> *They jest want this Californy*
> *— So's to lug new slave-states in*

> *To abuse ye, an' to scorn ye,*
> *— An' to plunder ye like sin.*

The war had barely begun, the summer of 1846, when a writer, Henry David Thoreau, who lived in Concord, Massachusetts, refused to pay his Massachusetts poll tax, denouncing the Mexican war. He was put in jail and spent one night there. His friends, without his consent, paid his tax, and he was released. Two years later, he gave a lecture, "Resistance to Civil Government," which was then printed as an essay, "Civil Disobedience":

> *It is not desirable to cultivate a respect for the law so much as for the right. … Law never made men a whit more just; and, by means of their respect for it, even the well-disposed are daily made the agents of injustice. A common and natural result of an undue respect for law is, that you may see a file of soldiers … marching in admirable order over hill and dale to the wars, against their wills, ay, against their common sense and consciences, which makes it very steep marching indeed, and produces a palpitation of the heart.*

His friend and fellow writer Ralph Waldo Emerson agreed, but thought it futile to protest. When Emerson visited Thoreau in jail and asked, "What are you doing in there?" it was reported that Thoreau replied, "What are you doing out there?"

The churches, for the most part, were either outspokenly for the war or timidly silent. The Reverend Theodore Parker, a Unitarian minister in Boston, combined eloquent criticism of the war with contempt for the Mexican people, whom he called "a wretched people; wretched in their origin, history and character," who must eventually give way as the Indians did. Yes, the United States should expand, he said, but not by war, rather by the power of her ideas, the pressure of her commerce, by "the steady advance of a superior race, with superior ideas and a better civilization. …"

The racism of Parker was widespread. Congressman Delano of Ohio, an antislavery Whig, opposed the war because he was afraid of Americans mingling with an inferior people who "embrace all shades of color … a sad compound of Spanish, English, Indian, and negro bloods … and resulting, it is said, in the production of a slothful, ignorant race of beings."

As the war went on, opposition grew. The American Peace Society printed a newspaper, the *Advocate of Peace*, which published poems, speeches, petitions, sermons against the war, and eyewitness accounts of the degradation of army life and the horrors of battle. Considering the strenuous efforts of the nation's leaders to build patriotic support, the amount of open dissent and criticism was remarkable. Antiwar meetings took place in spite of attacks by patriotic mobs.

As the army moved closer to Mexico City, the antislavery newspaper *The Liberator* daringly declared its wishes for the defeat of the American forces: "Every lover of Freedom and humanity, throughout the world, must wish them [the Mexicans] the most triumphant success. ..."

Frederick Douglass, a former slave and an extraordinary speaker and writer, wrote in his Rochester newspaper the *North Star*, January 21, 1848, of "the present disgraceful, cruel, and iniquitous war with our sister republic. Mexico seems a doomed victim to Anglo Saxon cupidity and love of dominion." Douglass was scornful of the unwillingness of opponents of the war to take real action (even the abolitionists kept paying their taxes):

> No politician of any considerable distinction or eminence seems willing to hazard his popularity with his party ... by an open and unqualified disapprobation of the war. None seem willing to take their stand for peace at all risks; and all seem willing that the war should be carried on, in some form or other.

Where was popular opinion? It is hard to say. After the first rush, enlistments began to dwindle. Historians of the Mexican war have

---

"We must march from Texas straight to the Pacific ocean, and be bounded only by its roaring wave. ... It is the destiny of the white race, it is the destiny of the Anglo-Saxon race. ..."

---

talked easily about "the people" and "public opinion." Their evidence, however, is not from "the people" but from the newspapers, claiming to be the voice of the people. The *New York Herald* wrote in August 1845: "The multitude cry aloud for war." The *New York Morning News* said "young and ardent spirits that throng the cities ... want but a direction to their restless energies, and their attention is already fixed on Mexico."

It is impossible to know the extent of popular support of the war. But there is evidence that many organized workingmen opposed the war. There were demonstrations of Irish workers in New York, Boston, and Lowell against the annexation of Texas. In May, when the war against Mexico began, New York workingmen called a meeting to oppose the war, and many Irish workers came. The meeting called the war a plot by slave owners and asked for the withdrawal of American troops from disputed territory. That year, a convention of the New England Workingmen's Association condemned the war and announced they would "not take up arms to sustain the Southern slaveholder in robbing one-fifth of our countrymen of their labor."

Some newspapers, at the very start of the war, protested. Horace Greeley wrote in the *New York Tribune*, May 12, 1846:

> We can easily defeat the armies of Mexico, slaughter them by thousands. ... Who believes that a score of victories over Mexico, the "annexation" of half her provinces, will give us more Liberty, a purer Morality, a more prosperous Industry, than we now have? ... Is not Life miserable enough, comes not Death soon enough, without resort to the hideous enginery of War?

The Recruits

What of those who fought the war—the soldiers who marched, sweated, got sick, died? The Mexican soldiers. The American soldiers. We know little of the reactions of Mexican soldiers. We know much more about the American army—volunteers, not conscripts, lured by money and opportunity for social advancement via promotion in the armed forces. Half of General Taylor's army were recent immigrants—Irish and German mostly. Their patriotism was not very strong. Indeed, many of them deserted to the Mexican side, enticed by money. Some enlisted in the Mexican army and formed their own battalion, the San Patricio (St. Patrick's) Battalion.

At first there seemed to be enthusiasm in the army, fired by pay and patriotism. Martial spirit was high in New York, where the legislature authorized the governor to call 50,000 volunteers. Placards read "Mexico or Death." There was a mass meeting of 20,000 people in Philadelphia. Three thousand volunteered in Ohio.

This initial spirit soon wore off. One young man wrote anonymously to the *Cambridge Chronicle*:

> *Neither have I the least idea of "joining" you, or in any way assisting the unjust war waging against Mexico. I have no wish to participate in such "glorious" butcheries of women and children as were displayed in the capture of Monterey, etc. Neither have I any desire to place myself under the dictation of a petty military tyrant, to every caprice of whose will I must yield implicit obedience. No sir-ee! ... Human butchery has had its day. ... And the time is rapidly approaching when the professional soldier will be placed on the same level as a bandit, the Bedouin, and the Thug.*

"The universal Yankee nation can regenerate and disenthrall the people of Mexico in a few years; and we believe it is part of our destiny to civilize that beautiful country."

There were extravagant promises and outright lies to build up the volunteer units. A man who wrote a history of the New York Volunteers declared: "Many enlisted for the sake of their families, having no employment, and having been offered 'three months' advance,' and were promised that they could leave part of their pay for their families to draw in their absence. ... I boldly pronounce, that the whole Regiment was got up by fraud."

By late 1846, recruitment was falling off, so physical requirements were lowered, and anyone bringing in acceptable recruits would get two dollars a head. Even this didn't work. Congress in early 1847 authorized 10 new regiments of regulars, to serve for the duration of the war, promising them 100 acres of public land upon honorable discharge. But dissatisfaction continued.

The Reality Battle

And soon, the reality of battle came in upon the glory and the promises. On the Rio Grande before Matamoros, as a Mexican army of 5,000 under General Arista faced Taylor's army of 3,000, the shells began to fly, and artilleryman Samuel French saw his first death in battle. John Weems describes it: "He happened to be staring at a man on horseback nearby when he saw a shot rip off the pommel of the saddle, tear through the man's body, and burst out with a crimson gush on the other side."

When the battle was over, 500 Mexicans were dead or wounded. There were perhaps 50 American casualties. Weems describes the aftermath: "Night blanketed weary men who fell asleep where they dropped on the trampled prairie grass, while around them other prostrate men from both armies screamed and groaned in agony from wounds. By the eerie light of torches the surgeon's saw was going the livelong night."

Away from the battlefield, in army camps, the romance of the recruiting posters was quickly forgotten. The 2nd Regiment of Mississippi Rifles, moving into New Orleans, was stricken by cold and sickness. The regimental surgeon reported: "Six months after our regiment had entered the service we had sustained a loss of 167 by death, and 134 by discharges." The regiment was packed into the holds of transports, 800 men into three ships. The surgeon continued:

The dark cloud of disease still hovered over us. The holds of the ships … were soon crowded with the sick. The effluvia was intolerable. … The sea became rough. … Through the long dark night the rolling ship would dash the sick man from side to side bruising his flesh upon the rough corners of his berth. The wild screams of the delirious, the lamentations of the sick, and the melancholy groans of the dying, kept up one continual scene of confusion. … Four weeks we were confined to the loathsome ships and before we had landed at the Brasos, we consigned 28 of our men to the dark waves.

Meanwhile, by land and by sea, Anglo-American forces were moving into California. A young naval officer, after the long voyage around the southern cape of South America, and up the coast to Monterey in California, wrote in his diary:

Asia … will be brought to our very doors. Population will flow into the fertile regions of California. The resources of the entire country … will be developed. … The public lands lying along the route [of railroads] will be changed from deserts into gardens, and a large population will be settled. …

It was a separate war that went on in California, where Anglo-Americans raided Spanish settlements, stole horses, and declared California separated from Mexico—the "Bear Flag Republic." Indians lived there, and naval officer Revere gathered the Indian chiefs and spoke to them (as he later recalled):

I have called you together to have a talk with you. The country you inhabit no longer belongs to Mexico, but to a mighty nation whose territory extends from the great ocean you have all seen or heard of, to another great ocean thousands of miles toward the rising sun. … Our armies are now in Mexico, and will soon conquer the whole country. But you have nothing to fear from us, if you do what is right … if you are faithful to your new rulers. … I hope you will alter your habits, and be industrious and frugal, and give up all the low vices which you practice. … We shall watch over you, and give you true liberty; but beware of sedition, lawlessness, and all other crimes, for the army which shields can assuredly punish, and it will reach you in your most retired hiding places.

> *"It is not desirable to cultivate a respect for the law so much as for the right."*

General Kearny moved easily into New Mexico, and Santa Fe was taken without battle. An American staff officer described the reaction of the Mexican population to the U.S. Army's entrance into the capital city:

Our march into the city … was extremely warlike, with drawn sabers, and daggers in every look. … As the American flag was raised, and the cannon boomed its glorious national salute from the hill, the pent-up emotion of many of the women could be suppressed no longer … as the wail of grief arose above the din of our horses' tread, and reached our ears from the depth of the gloomy-looking buildings on every hand.

That was in August. In December, Mexicans in Taos, New Mexico, rebelled against American rule. The revolt was put down and arrests were made. But many of the rebels fled and carried on sporadic attacks, killing a number of Americans, then hiding in the mountains. The American army pursued, and in a final desperate battle, in which 600 to 700 rebels were engaged, 150 were killed, and it seemed the rebellion was now over.

In Los Angeles, too, there was a revolt. Mexicans forced the American garrison there to surrender in September 1846. The United States did not retake Los Angeles until January, after a bloody battle.

General Taylor had moved across the Rio Grande, occupied Matamoros, and now moved southward through Mexico. But his volunteers became more unruly on Mexican territory. Mexican villages were pillaged by drunken troops. Cases of rape began to multiply.

As the soldiers moved up the Rio Grande to Camargo, the heat became unbearable, the water impure, and sickness grew—diarrhea, dysentery, and other maladies—until 1,000 were dead. At first the dead were buried to the sounds of the "Dead March" played by a military band. Then the number of dead was too great, and formal military funerals ceased. Southward to Monterey and another battle, where men and horses died in agony, and one officer described the ground as "slippery with … foam and blood."

The U.S. Navy bombarded Veracruz in an indiscriminate killing of civilians. One of the Navy's shells hit the post office, another a surgical hospital. In two days, 1,300 shells were fired into the city, until it surrendered. A reporter for the *New Orleans Delta* wrote: "The Mexicans variously estimate their loss at from 500 to 1,000 killed and wounded, but all agree that the loss among the soldiery is comparatively small and the destruction among the women and children is very great."

Colonel Hitchcock, coming into the city, wrote: "I shall never forget the horrible fire of our mortars … going with dreadful certainty … often in the centre of private dwellings—it was awful. I shudder to think of it." Still, Hitchcock, the dutiful

> *"I shall never forget the horrible fire of our mortars … going with dreadful certainty … often in the centre of private dwellings — it was awful. I shudder to think of it."*

soldier, wrote for General Scott "a sort of address to the Mexican people" which was then printed in English and Spanish by the tens of thousands saying "we have not a particle of ill-will towards you … we are here for no earthly purpose except the hope of obtaining a peace."

It was a war of the American elite against the Mexican elite, each side exhorting, using, killing its own population as well as the other. The Mexican commander Santa Anna had crushed rebellion after rebellion, his troops also raping and plundering after victory. When Col. Hitchcock and Gen. Winfield Scott moved into Santa Anna's estate, they found its walls full of ornate paintings. But half his army was dead or wounded.

General Scott moved toward the last battle—for Mexico City—with 10,000 soldiers. They were not anxious for battle. Three days' march from Mexico City, at Jalapa, seven of his eleven regiments evaporated, their enlistment times up, the reality of battle and disease too much for them.

On the outskirts of Mexico City, at Churubusco, Mexican and American armies clashed for three hours and thousands died on both sides. Among the Mexicans taken prisoner were sixty-nine U.S. Army deserters.

As often in war, battles were fought without point. After one such engagement near Mexico City, with terrible casualties, a marine lieutenant blamed Gen. Scott: "He had originated it in error and caused it to be fought, with inadequate forces, for an object that had no existence."

In the final battle for Mexico City, Anglo-American troops took the height of Chapultepec and entered the city of 200,000 people, General Santa Anna having moved northward. This was September 1847. A Mexican merchant wrote to a friend about the bombardment of the city: "In some cases whole blocks were destroyed and a great number of men, women and children killed and wounded."

General Santa Anna fled to Huamantla, where another battle was fought, and he had to flee again. An American infantry lieutenant wrote to his parents what happened after an officer named Walker was killed in battle:

> General Lane … told us to "avenge the death of the gallant Walker" … Grog shops were broken open first, and then, maddened with liquor, every species of outrage was committed. Old women and girls were stripped of their clothing—and many suffered still greater outrages. Men were shot by dozens … their property, churches, stores, and dwelling houses ransacked. … It made me for the first time ashamed of my country.

One Pennsylvania volunteer, stationed at Matamoros late in the war, wrote:

> We are under very strict discipline here. Some of our officers are very good men but the balance of them are very tyrannical and brutal toward the men. … [T]onight on drill an officer laid a soldier's skull open with his sword. … But the time may come and that soon when officers and men will stand on equal footing. … A soldier's life is very disgusting.

On the night of August 15, 1847, volunteer regiments from Virginia, Mississippi, and North Carolina rebelled in northern Mexico against Col. Robert Treat Paine. Paine killed a mutineer, but two of his lieutenants refused to help him quell the mutiny. The rebels were ultimately exonerated in an attempt to keep the peace.

Desertion grew. In March 1847 the army reported over a thousand deserters. The total number of deserters during the war was 9,207 (5,331 regulars and 3,876 volunteers). Those who did not desert became harder and harder to manage. General Cushing referred to 65 such men in the 1st Regiment of Massachusetts Infantry as "incorrigibly mutinous and insubordinate."

The glory of victory was for the president and the generals, not the deserters, the dead, the wounded. The Massachusetts Volunteers had started with 630 men. They came home with 300 dead, mostly from disease, and at the reception dinner on their return their commander, General Cushing, was hissed by his men.

As the veterans returned home, speculators immediately showed up to buy the land warrants given by the government. Many of the soldiers, desperate for money, sold their 160 acres for less than 50 dollars.

Mexico surrendered. There were calls among Americans to take all of Mexico. The Treaty of Guadalupe Hidalgo, signed February 1848, just took half. The Texas boundary was set at the Rio Grande; New Mexico and California were ceded. The United States paid Mexico $15 million, which led the *Whig Intelligencer* to conclude that "we take nothing by conquest. … Thank God." ■

Used by permission of Howard Zinn. This reading is excerpted from A People's History of the United States *(teaching edition), by Howard Zinn (New York: The New Press, 1997).*

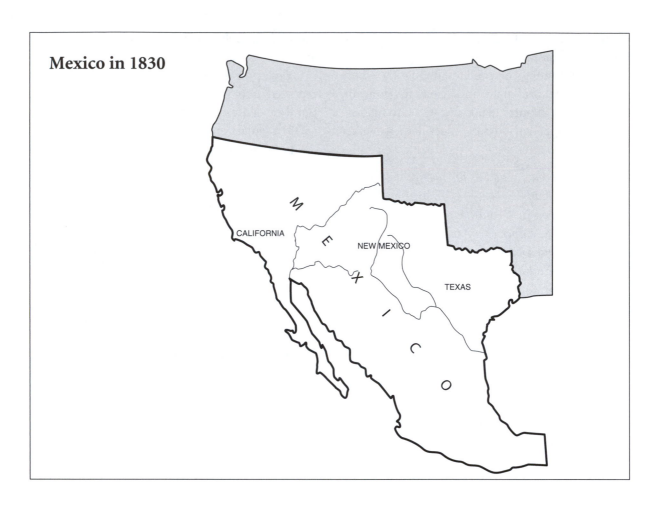

Mexico in 1830

CALIFORNIA

M
E
X
I
C
O

NEW MEXICO

TEXAS

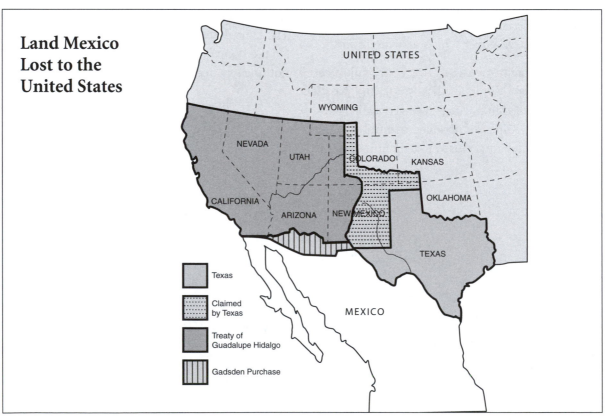

Land Mexico Lost to the United States

UNITED STATES

WYOMING

NEVADA

UTAH

COLORADO

KANSAS

CALIFORNIA

ARIZONA

NEW MEXICO

OKLAHOMA

TEXAS

MEXICO

Texas

Claimed by Texas

Treaty of Guadalupe Hidalgo

Gadsden Purchase

War with Mexico

IN 1836 WHEN TEXAS DECLARED its independence from Mexico, white Southerners hoped to acquire Texas as a new slave state. Northerners feared that the admission of Texas to the Union would not only increase the South's power in Congress but would also embroil the United States in a war with Mexico. Nevertheless by 1845 enough politicians were caught up in the fervor of westward expansion—believing that it was the destiny of the nation to reach from shore to shore—that white Southern politicians were able to prevail in getting Texas admitted to the Union as the twenty-eighth state. Mexico was outraged at this action. After a border skirmish between American troops and Mexican troops, the United States declared war on Mexico in May 1846.

On February 2, 1848, after almost two years of fighting, the nations ended the war by signing the Treaty of Guadalupe Hidalgo. This treaty gave the United States vast new regions that today include California, Arizona, New Mexico, Utah, Nevada, and parts of Colorado and Wyoming. The fear that these territories would organize into states intensified the sectional conflict between the North and the South. Many Northerners opposed the extension of slavery even into the newly acquired lands that lay south of the line established by the Missouri Compromise. ■

—*from* American Odyssey *(2003). Glencoe/McGraw-Hill*

Reading Questions

1. What important perspectives are missing from this textbook passage?

2. How might this coverage of the war affect how students think about history or the world today?

Unsung Heroes

By Howard Zinn

A HIGH SCHOOL STUDENT recently confronted me: "I read in your book *A People's History of the United States* about the massacres of Indians, the long history of racism, the persistence of poverty in the richest country in the world, the senseless wars. How can I keep from being thoroughly alienated and depressed?"

It's a question I've heard many times before. Another question often put to me by students is: Don't we need our national idols? You are taking down all our national heroes—the Founding Fathers, Andrew Jackson, Abraham Lincoln, Theodore Roosevelt, Woodrow Wilson, John F. Kennedy.

Granted, it is good to have historical figures we can admire and emulate. But why hold up as models the 55 rich white men who drafted the Constitution as a way of establishing a government that would protect the interests of their class—slaveholders, merchants, bondholders, land speculators?

Why not recall the humanitarianism of William Penn, an early colonist who made peace with the Delaware Indians instead of warring on them, as other colonial leaders were doing?

Why not John Woolman, who in the years before the Revolution refused to pay taxes to support the British wars, and who spoke out against slavery?

Osceola, Seminole leader, led a successful resistance of Native Americans and escaped African slaves against U.S. troops.

Why not Capt. Daniel Shays, veteran of the Revolutionary War, who led a revolt of poor farmers in Western Massachusetts against the oppressive taxes levied by the rich who controlled the Massachusetts Legislature?

Why go along with the hero-worship, so universal in our history textbooks, of Andrew Jackson, the slave owner, the killer of Indians? Jackson was the architect of the Trail of Tears, which resulted in the deaths of 4,000 of 16,000 Cherokees who were kicked off their land in Georgia and sent into exile in Oklahoma.

Why not replace him as national icon with John Ross, a Cherokee chief who resisted the dispossession of his people, and whose wife died on the Trail of Tears? Or the Seminole leader Osceola, imprisoned and finally killed for leading a guerrilla campaign against the removal of the Indians?

And while we're at it, should not the Lincoln Memorial be joined by a memorial to Frederick Douglass, who better represented the struggle against slavery? It was that crusade of black and white abolitionists, growing into a great national movement, that pushed a reluctant Lincoln into finally issuing a halfhearted Emancipation Proclamation, and persuaded Congress to pass the 13th, 14th, and 15th amendments.

Take another presidential hero, Theodore Roosevelt, who is always near the top of the tiresome lists of Our Greatest Presidents. There he is on Mount Rushmore, as a permanent reminder of our historical amnesia about his racism, his militarism, his love of war.

Why not replace him as hero—granted, removing him from Mount Rushmore will take some doing—with Mark Twain? Roosevelt, remember, had congratulated an American general who in 1906 ordered the massacre of 600 men, women, and children on a Philippine island. As vice president of the Anti-Imperialist League, Twain denounced this and continued to point out the cruelties committed in the Philippine war under the slogan, "My country, right or wrong."

As for Woodrow Wilson, another honored figure in the pantheon of American liberalism, shouldn't we remind his admirers that he insisted on racial segregation in federal buildings, that he bombarded the Mexican coast, sent an occupation army into Haiti and the Dominican Republic, brought our country into the hell of World War I, and put antiwar protesters in prison?

Should we not bring forward as a national hero Emma Goldman, one of those Wilson sent to prison, or Helen Keller, who fearlessly spoke out against the war?

And enough worship of John F. Kennedy, a Cold Warrior who began the covert war in Indochina, went along with the planned invasion of Cuba, and was slow to act against racial segregation in the South.

Should we not replace the portraits of our presidents, which too often take up all the space on our classroom walls, with the likenesses of grassroots heroes like Fannie Lou Hamer, the Mississippi sharecropper? Mrs. Hamer was evicted from her farm and tortured in prison after she joined the Civil Rights Movement, but

Helen Keller was a socialist and advocate for workers' rights. "Why in this land of great wealth is there such great poverty?" she wrote in 1912.

she became an eloquent voice for freedom. Or with Ella Baker, whose wise counsel and support guided the young Black people who joined the Student Nonviolent Coordinating Committee, the militant edge of the Civil Rights Movement in the Deep South?

In the year 1992, the quincentennial of the arrival of Columbus in this hemisphere, there were meetings all over the country to celebrate him, but also, for the first time, to challenge the customary exaltation of the Great Discoverer. I was at a symposium in New Jersey where I pointed to the terrible crimes against the indigenous people of Hispaniola committed by Columbus and his fellow explorers. Afterward, the other man on the platform, who was chairman of the New Jersey Columbus Day celebration, said to me: "You don't understand—we Italian Americans need our heroes." Yes, I understood the desire for heroes, I said, but why choose a murderer and kidnapper for such an honor? Why not choose Joe DiMaggio, or Toscanini, or Fiorello LaGuardia, or Sacco and Vanzetti? (The man was not persuaded.)

Should we not bring forward as a national hero Emma Goldman, one of those Wilson sent to prison, or Helen Keller, who fearlessly spoke out against the war?

The same misguided values that have made slaveholders, Indian-killers, and militarists the heroes of our history books still operate today. We have heard Sen. John McCain, Republican of Arizona, repeatedly referred to as a war hero. Yes, we must sympathize with McCain's ordeal as a war prisoner in Vietnam, where he endured cruelties. But must we call someone a hero who participated in the invasion of a far-off country and dropped bombs on men, women, and children?

I have come across only one voice in the mainstream press daring to dissent from the general admiration for McCain—that of the poet, novelist, and *Boston Globe* columnist James Carroll. Carroll contrasted the heroism of McCain, the warrior, to that of Philip Berrigan, who has gone to prison dozens of times for protesting the war in Vietnam

and the dangerous nuclear arsenal maintained by the U.S. government. Carroll wrote: "Berrigan, in jail, is the truly free man, while McCain remains imprisoned in an unexamined sense of martial honor."

Our country is full of heroic people who are not presidents or military leaders or Wall Street wizards, but who are doing something to keep alive the spirit of resistance to injustice and war.

I think of Kathy Kelly and all those other people from Voices in the Wilderness who, in defiance of federal law, traveled to Iraq more than a dozen times to bring food and medicine to people suffering under the U.S.-imposed sanctions.

I think also of the thousands of students on more than 100 college campuses across the country who are protesting their universities' connection with sweatshop-produced apparel.

I think of the four McDonald sisters in Minneapolis, all nuns, who have gone to jail repeatedly for protesting against the Alliant Corporation's production of land mines.

I think, too, of the thousands of people who have traveled to Fort Benning, Ga., to demand the closing of the murderous School of the Americas.

I think of the West Coast longshoremen who participated in an eight-hour work stoppage to protest the death sentence levied against Mumia Abu-Jamal.

And so many more.

We all know individuals—most of them unsung, unrecognized—who have, often in the most modest ways, spoken out or acted on their beliefs for a more egalitarian, more just, peace-loving society.

To ward off alienation and gloom, it is only necessary to remember the unremembered heroes of the past, and to look around us for the unnoticed heroes of the present. ■

Reprinted by permission from The Progressive, *409 E Main St, Madison, WI 53703. www.progressive.org*

Teaching About Unsung Heroes

Encouraging students to appreciate those who fought for social justice

SCHOOLS HELP TEACH students who "we" are. And as Howard Zinn points out in his essay "Unsung Heroes" (see p. 51), too often the curricular "we" are the great slaveholders, plunderers, imperialists, and captains of industry of yesteryear.

Thus when we teach about the genocide Columbus launched against the Taínos, or Washington's scorched-earth war on the Iroquois, or even Abraham Lincoln's promise in his first inaugural address to support a constitutional amendment making slavery permanent in Southern states, some students may experience this new information as a personal loss. In part, as Zinn suggests, this is because they've been denied a more honorable past with which to identify—one that acknowledges racism and exploitation, but also highlights courageous initiatives for social equality and justice.

One of the best and most diverse collections of writing I have received from my sophomore U.S. history students was generated from a project aimed to get students to appreciate those "other Americans." From time to time over the years, I've had students do research on people in history who worked for justice. But these were often tedious exercises and, despite my coaxing and pleading, student writing ended up sounding encyclopedia-like.

An idea to revise this assignment came to me while reading Stephen O'Connor's curricular memoir, *Will My Name Be Shouted Out?*, about his

I wanted these students-as-historical-activists to meet each other and learn a bit about each other's life work.

experiences teaching writing to junior high school students in New York City. O'Connor was captivated by August Wilson's monologues in his play *Fences.* He read some of these aloud to his students and offered them a wide-open prompt: "Write a monologue in which a parent tells his or her life story to a child."

It struck me that I might get much more passionate, imaginative writing about the lives of social justice activists if I offered students a similar assignment. Instead of asking them to stand outside their research subjects and write in the third person, I invited them to attempt to become those individuals at the end of their lives. Students could construct their papers as meditations about their individuals' accomplishments and possibly their regrets. They might narrate parts of their lives to a child, a younger colleague, or even to a reporter.

I decided to launch this project out of a unit I do that looks at the sometimes-tense relationship between the abolitionist movement and the women's rights movement in the years before and right after the Civil War. I framed it as the "Racial and Gender Justice Project: People Who Made Change." Because this would likely be the only time during the year that I would structure an entire research project around the lives of individual social justice activists, I wanted to give students an opportunity to learn about people throughout U.S. history, not

Dolores Huerta was a co-founder of the United Farm Workers. She was especially active in organizing against the use of pesticides in the fields that were poisoning workers and their children.

simply during the decades between the 1830s and 1860s. I was aware that this presented something of a problem, as students wouldn't yet have the historical context to fully appreciate the work of, say, Dolores Huerta or Emma Goldman. But their reading would alert them to themes and events that we would cover later, and I could fill in some of the blank spots in their knowledge as they completed their research.

I remember one year writing up and assigning a choice-list of activists for students to research. I reviewed them in class one by one, talking briefly about their work and accomplishments. Can you spell b-o-r-i-n-g? This time I decided to write up short first-person roles for students to "try on" in class and to meet each other in character. I wasn't very scientific in the choices of activists that I offered students—in fact, some, like Bessie Smith, fell a bit awkwardly into the "activist" category. I tried for racial and

> *Instead of asking them to stand outside their research subjects and write in the third person, I invited them to attempt to become those individuals.*

gender diversity; I also tried to mix the famous with the not-so-famous, mostly concentrating on people who worked in social movements. (If the activists were too "unsung," students would have difficulty finding out enough about them to complete the writing. See box with complete list on p. 59.) My list was unavoidably idiosyncratic and missed lots of worthy individuals. However, in the end, if none of the people I included excited students, they could propose alternatives.

I wanted the roles I wrote up to be short and provocative. The point was not to do the assignment for students but to lure them into the activists' lives. Because my students are mostly white—and with this group (my only U.S. History class), overwhelmingly male—I wanted to make sure that at least several of the social justice activists were white men. It was important that the young white men in class know that people who look like they do have not only been the slave owners and land-grabbers, they have also been part of a rainbow of resistance in U.S. history. Here are a couple of typical roles (the entire list is archived on the Rethinking Schools website, http://www.rethinkingschools.org/ archive/15_01/role151.shtml):

Abolitionist John Brown

- **John Brown:** People have called me crazy because I, a white man, gave up my life in the cause to free enslaved black people. I fought in what was called "bloody Kansas" to make sure that Kansas did not enter the United States as a slave state. And it's true, I killed people there. But it was a just cause, and I took no pleasure in killing. I'm most famous for leading the attack on the U.S. arsenal at Harper's Ferry, Va. In one sense my mission failed, because we were captured and I was executed. But I am convinced that my actions hastened the day of freedom for the people who had been enslaved.

- **Fannie Lou Hamer:** I was the youngest of 20 children. After I married, I was a share-cropper in Mississippi for 18 years. I risked my life when I registered to vote in 1962. I'd

had enough of poverty. I'd had enough of racism. I began to organize for our rights, by working with SNCC, the Student Nonviolent Coordinating Committee. In the summer of 1964, I traveled to the Democratic National Convention where I was a representative of the Mississippi Freedom Democratic Party, which we'd created because the regular Democratic Party wouldn't allow blacks to participate. I sang "Go Tell It on the Mountain," and asked the now-famous question: "Is this America?"

In class, I briefly described the project and distributed a card with one role description to each student. I gave them a few minutes to trade cards if they felt like it, but I emphasized that ultimately they weren't limited to researching the person on the card they drew; they would be able to choose someone else if they liked. I wanted these students-as-historical-activists to meet each other and learn a bit about each other's life work. Once they'd settled on an individual, I distributed "Hello, My Name Is …" stickers and had them write down and wear their names prominently, so other students would be able to easily see who was who. Finally, I gave each of them a "Racial and Gender Justice Hunt" sheet. In the "hunt," students had tasks, such as: "Find someone in the group who has spent time in jail for their activities or beliefs (or would have if they'd been caught). What happened?" I required them to use a different person in their answers to each question, so they needed to keep circulating among other class members to complete the assignment. This was a delightful activity, filled with laughter and energy.

The following day we circled-up to review some of the questions and talk over what they had learned about the different individuals. Before we headed for the library to begin research, I gave the students an assignment sheet: "Choose an individual who stood up for racial or gender justice. Perhaps this individual worked to end slavery, for women's right to own property or to vote, for farmworkers' rights, or to integrate schools in the South. You needn't agree with everything this person stood for or agree with how he or she went about working for change. The only requirements are that the person tried to make this a better place to live and also significantly affected society. You may choose an individual (or group) who attended the 'getting to know you' gathering we did in class or come up with one of your own. If you choose one on your own, check with me first."

"The better educated didn't like me because I was so good at what I did, and I loved speaking out to people. I can't read a book, but I can read the people."

I told them that they were going to be writing about their individual in the first person, but I didn't want to describe the full assignment until they had read and collected stories.

For their library and outside-of-class research, I gave students written research guidelines: "Find out as much about your individual as you can. Try to answer the following questions—and be sure to look for specific stories from their lives:

1. What significant events in this person's life shaped their social commitment? What happened in their life to make them willing to take the risks they took?

2. What did the person want to accomplish or change?

3. What did they accomplish?

4. What methods did this person use to try to effect change?

5. What, if anything, about their life reminds you of something in your life? Is there anything in their life that you relate to, or that is similar to feelings or experiences you've had?

6. What meaning does this person's life have for today?

7. Find at least three quotes from the individual that you agree with or think are somehow significant.

I told them that they would need to turn in full answers to these questions with their final write-up.

Not surprisingly, some students had an easier time than others. The student doing Elaine Brown, one-time leader of the Black Panther Party, had trouble finding anything on her life and, unfortunately, didn't have the energy to read the entirety of Brown's compelling book, *A Taste of Power*, so moved on to Elizabeth Cady Stanton. But by and large students were able to discover lots about their activists.

Grandma T. and Other Stories

I've found that it's always better to show students what I'm looking for, rather than just tell them. So I save student papers from year to year to use as examples. My student Wakisha Weekly virtually *became* Sojourner Truth in a paper she had written for me in a previous year. I read it to the class to demonstrate the kind of intimacy, detail, and voice that I hoped students would strive for. She structured it as a conversation between a dying Sojourner Truth and her granddaughter. It opened:

> *"Grandma T., how are you?"*
>
> *"Oh, I am fine, baby doll. As fine as you can be in a hospital bed with all of these tubes."*
>
> *"Are you going to die, Grandma?"*
>
> *"I'm not going to die, honey. I'm going home like a shooting star."*
>
> *"Can you tell me a story, Grandma?"*

Wakisha's "Grandma T." tells her granddaughter about life in slavery, being sold when her master died and of life with successive owners. She talks of her escape and her conversion:

> *"Later in my life is when I felt a powerful force. It was God all around me. God gave me the name Sojourner and told me to move to New York and to speak to people. I called it preaching. I often put people in tears. The better educated didn't like me because I was*

so good at what I did, and I loved speaking out to people. I can't read a book, but I can read the people."

"You don't know how to read, Grandma?"

"No, I was never taught. Slaves didn't go to school or to college to be educated. The masters thought you were there just to work for them."

"But Grandma, I love to read, and I am really good at it."

"That's good, baby. And part of the reason you can read and go to school is because women didn't like to be put down by the men and wanted to work, earn money, and even go to school. So we stood up for ourselves."

"Who is we, Grandma T.?"

Sojourner Truth

Wakisha used the granddaughter's questions to pull her narrative along. In response to questions and comments, Grandma T. continued to tell the history, weaving her personal story with movement history—both the abolitionist and women's rights movements.

After hearing Wakisha's piece, students and I talked about what they liked about it and what made the writing both interesting and informative. We followed by brainstorming ways that we could write about the lives of our racial and gender justice activists. They came up with excellent ideas, including: students going to a nursing home to interview someone for a class project; a letter to a loved one, saying what you never got to say during your life; two lifelong friends walking and talking about the activities they participated in together.

I didn't want students to run simply with the first thing that came into their heads, so for homework I asked them to write two different introductions to their piece. We began these in class and the next day they brought them in and read them to one another in pairs. I asked people to nominate exemplary openings that they heard so that these could be shared with the entire class and broaden our sampling of possible approaches.

What students ultimately produced sounded nothing like an encyclopedia. Andy wrote a story about "Nicholas," a former member of the Massachusetts 54th, the first regiment of black soldiers in American history. Drawing largely on letters in the book *A Grand Army of Black Men* (edited by Edwin S. Redkey), Andy set his piece in a facility for seniors, many years after the Civil War. Nicholas is sitting with his regular breakfast companion, Susan, who asks him at long last about the part of his ear that is missing. "To know about my ear, I would have to tell you a story," and launches into a richly detailed tale about his decision to volunteer for the 54th and his experiences fighting in South Carolina.

Tyler's Marcus Garvey lies on his deathbed wondering whether or not he did enough for racial equality. He flashes back to his impoverished Jamaican childhood: "Though we had close to no money, we had heart, and each other."

Jennifer patterned her story about Rosa Parks on Wakisha's Grandma T. In an interior monologue, Jeff's Malcolm X reflected on how he changed, and what he feared and hoped for, while sitting in a hotel room the day before his final speech at the Audubon Ballroom. Jonathan wrote an unusual and complex piece that began on the day Leonard Peltier was released from prison—a day that is still in the future. His daughter tells the story of how she became an activist for Native American rights after listening to her father narrate a videotape-letter to her about why he can't be with her as she grows up.

Tyler's Marcus Garvey lies on his deathbed wondering whether or not he did enough for racial equality.

Gina wrote an utterly authentic-feeling story about two young children who visit César Chávez for a class project. In her story, Chávez narrates episodes from La Causa:

"The fight was not over. In 1968, I fasted—that means I didn't eat anything—for 25 days. A different time I fasted for 24 days, and again I fasted, this time for 36 days. You know how hungry you can get when you miss breakfast or lunch—but imagine missing 36 breakfasts, lunches, and dinners."

"But Mr. Chávez, didn't you ever fight? Like punch them or anything?" Richard asked.

"No, no! Violence isn't right. Everything can be done without hurting somebody else. You can always show people your side with words or pictures or actions. Hurting somebody to make your point is wrong, and it never needs to be done. We never punched anyone, even if they punched us first. We just stayed at our place and showed them that they couldn't stop us."

"That's really neat, Mr. Chávez! I'm gonna do that," Linda said determinedly.

People Who Made Change

Frederick Douglass

Harriet Tubman

John Brown

Soldier of the 54th Massachusetts Regiment

Elizabeth Gurley Flynn

César Chávez

Sojourner Truth

Jeannette Rankin

Malcolm X

Elizabeth Cady Stanton

Susan B. Anthony

Carlos Bulosan

William Lloyd Garrison

Sarah and Angelina Grimké

Emma Goldman

Elaine Brown

Marcus Garvey

Black Panther Party for Self Defense Member

Jackie Robinson

Rosa Parks

Bessie Smith

Bernice Reagon

Queen Lili'uokalani

Nat Turner

Henry David Thoreau

Melba Pattillo Beals

Mickey Schwerner, James Cheney, and Andrew Goodman

Fannie Lou Hamer

Harvey Milk

Dolores Huerta

Fred Korematsu

Leonard Peltier

Harvey Milk was the first openly gay elected official in the United States. Milk was elected to the San Francisco Board of Supervisors in 1977. He and Mayor George Moscone were murdered in 1978 by a conservative city supervisor, Dan White.

> *In a myth-shattering history curriculum where heroes are regularly yanked from their pedestals, it's vital that we alert students to currents of generosity, solidarity, democracy, anti-racism, and social equality in the nation's past—and present.*

"I'm Gonna Do That"

In a myth-shattering history curriculum where heroes are regularly yanked from their pedestals, it's vital that we alert students to currents of generosity, solidarity, democracy, anti-racism, and social equality in the nation's past—and present. We don't need to make these up. They are there. Yes, we need to carefully analyze movements for change and acknowledge their shortcomings, the times they manifested those very characteristics that they sought to oppose in the larger society. And yes, we need to engage students in thinking about the relationship between strategies and aims, because not all activism is equally effective, and some can actually be counterproductive. But the curriculum that demands perfection will be filled with blank pages. As Howard Zinn emphasizes, there are countless individuals who have worked "to keep alive the spirit of resistance to injustice and war." Let's work concretely toward a curriculum of hope. Let's give students the opportunity to conclude: "I'm gonna do that." ■

This article first appeared in the Rethinking Schools book Rethinking Our Classrooms: Teaching for Equity and Justice, Vol. 2.

Racial and Gender Justice Hunt

Find someone in the group who:

1. Has spent time in jail for their activities or beliefs (or would have if they'd been caught). What happened?

2. Worked against slavery or other forms of racism. What exactly did they do?

3. Worked for women's rights, workers' rights, or for the rights of gays and lesbians. What did they do?

4. Believed it was necessary to use violence to achieve justice. What did they do?

5. Worked for justice nonviolently. What did they do?

6. You had never heard of before. What did they do? Why do you think you'd never heard of them?

7. You had heard of. What new thing(s) did you learn about this person?

8. Is a white person who worked for racial justice. What did they do?

Lawrence, 1912:
The Singing Strike

THIS ACTIVITY EMBODIES a couple of key insights of Howard Zinn's *A People's History of the United States*. One is that history is not inevitable. People's choices matter. Through role play, students in this lesson explore some of the actual dilemmas faced by strikers in Lawrence, Mass., in 1912. Here, the teaching methodology is designed to match the history itself, as students portray Industrial Workers of the World organizers deciding how—and for what—to conduct a massive strike. The other is that social class matters. Too often, traditional textbooks and curricula neglect the way social class has shaped our country's history and how people's understanding of class has influenced their actions. Social class is at the heart of this lesson, as it is at the heart of so much of Howard Zinn's work.

This activity—co-authored with Norm Diamond and included originally in the book *The Power in Our Hands: A Curriculum on the History of Work and Workers in the United States*—highlights how unions can have different goals and structures than the ones that predominate today. In "Lawrence, 1912," students contrast the American Federation of Labor and the Industrial Workers of the World. Students act as, and empathize with, union organizers. The role play illustrates, well, the power in our hands—one of the first major victories for U.S. labor, and an inspirational instance of worker solidarity. This lesson broadens students' sense of what workers can and do fight for beyond wages and benefits.

Goals/Objectives:

- Students will become familiar with different understandings of the function and purpose of labor unions.

- Students will see relationships between these different conceptions of unions and the actual organizations that were built.

- Students will learn about some of the practicalities of labor organizing.

- Students will practice collective decision-making.

Materials Needed:

- Student Handout: "You Are in the IWW"

- Student Handout: "Lawrence, 1912—Part 1: The Strike Is On!"

- Student Handout: "Lawrence Problem-Solving #1: Getting Organized"

- Student Handout: "Lawrence, 1912—Part 2: Unity in Diversity" (student copies optional)

- Student Handout: "Lawrence Problem-Solving #2: Can We Win?"

- Student Handout: "Lawrence, 1912—Part 3: The Outcome"

Time Required:

The duration of the role play depends in large part on how long students take when they assume the role of IWW members and discuss issues confronted by striking workers in Lawrence. Several class periods are required for students to get the most out of the activity. And, as mentioned in the introduction to this guide, the pedagogy here reinforces the historical knowledge: students grasp how "people make history" as they discuss the difficult choices faced by the actual participants. It's a history of living choices and not simply dead facts on a page.

Procedure:

Getting into Role

1. Distribute Student Handout "You Are in the IWW." Explain to students that they will be involved in a role play in which each of them will portray a member of the Industrial Workers of the World—the IWW. Therefore, it will be important that they fully understand their roles. Tell students that you will put them in small groups so that they can help one another and you can better assist them with their work. Encourage students to complete the AFL/IWW comparisons in as much detail as possible. If students have not written interior monologues before, it would be helpful to review this part of the assignment.

2. Form the groups and ask students to read the role and work on the AFL/IWW comparisons. They should work individually on the interior monologues.

3. Ask for a few volunteers to read their interior monologues, either in their small groups or to the entire class.

4. Review with students the IWW role:

   • What big changes have occurred in the workplace?

   • How were tools owned before? How are they owned in the workplace now?

   • What is a craft union?

   • What change has taken place in the ownership of industry?

   • How do all these changes affect the ability of unions to bargain for their members?

   • What kinds of workers does the AFL try to organize?

   • How does this compare to the IWW?

   • Remind them of Big Bill Haywood's metaphor of the hand from the reading. What was the point of Haywood's demonstration? How does the IWW try to bring the separate fingers into a fist? Is it simply that the IWW doesn't divide people by craft, as the AFL does? How is the kind of education and involvement encouraged of IWW members important in uniting workers?

   • What do IWW members think the goal of a union should be? (What kind of society do you want to create?)

   • Why do you sing together?

5. To clarify the reading up to this point, suggest that students imagine an industry producing a familiar product, such as shoes. Have them picture a number of shoe factories, set in different geographical locations. Ask how many owners there might have been in the 19th century. By 1912, if the number of factories stayed the same, would we expect more, fewer, or the same number of owners? If there had been a union in one of the factories at an earlier time, and the same union existed in 1912, how would the concentration of ownership have affected it? [It could be placed in competition with other workers in other factories of the same owner. Now if it went on strike, the company could shift production and obtain the same products or even increase production at its other factories.] Inside the factory, how have tools changed? Are there different kinds of workers? What would the IWW do about the changes in working conditions?

6. Remind students they are IWW members and interview them about their ideas. Play

this part with a contentious attitude, acting more as "devil's advocate" than as neutral questioner. Pose these questions as challenges:

- Why do you think women can be organized?

- How can immigrant groups that don't even speak the same language get together in a union?

- What makes you think that the whole society can be changed? What makes you believe that lowly, unskilled workers are in any position to change society?

- If you don't recognize the right of owners to own, how could anything even be produced? Who would get everybody organized and working?

- If the AFL is so bad, why does it have so many more members around the country than the IWW?

Organizing for the Strike

1. Explain to students that as IWW members, they are going to be part of an important strike involving thousands of people. Their goal is both to build a strike that can win and to build a union in line with the IWW principles they've read about and discussed. Before talking about the specific strike, we need to discuss how to accomplish our larger, long-term goals: to build a union where all the members are leaders as well as organizers for social change.

2. Write on the board or overhead the following quote from Eugene V. Debs, a founder of the IWW:

Too long have the workers of the world waited for some Moses to lead them out of bondage. He has not come; he never will come. I would not lead you out if I could; for if you could be led out, you could be led back again. I would have you make up your minds that there is nothing that you cannot do for yourselves.

Read this aloud with the class. Ask them:

- What would people have to believe about themselves in order to accept that paragraph?

- What attitudes would organizers need to develop and help others develop? (Some possible answers include: that we can act on our convictions; that we are able to join with others; that our actions together can make a difference.)

- List student contributions on the board.

3. Distribute Student Handout "Lawrence, 1912—Part 1" and "Lawrence Problem-Solving #1". Read the selections aloud in class. Ask them to jot down ideas for each of the questions in the problem solving.

Strikers' children, Lawrence, Mass., 1912.

The Strike Is On

1. Review with students:

- Why did the strike occur? Besides the immediate events, the speed-up and pay cut, what about working and living conditions was important in the decision to strike?

- What obstacles face IWW organizers attempting to build a unified strike? What divisions might exist within the workforce or community? What attitudes toward authority?

- Why did the AFL act as it did?

2. Remind students that they are IWW members, planning and leading a complicated struggle. Once again, their goal is not simply to win the strike (although that's important), but to build a union along the principles of the IWW. The first problems they will face are included in "Lawrence Problem-Solving #1." Even before that, however, they'll have to decide on the process they'll use to discuss and solve the problems.

3. Seat students in a circle so that they can talk to one another more easily. Explain that because theirs is a democratic union and because they believe in equality, no one will be around to tell them what to do. In the IWW, not only would they not allow a single individual to make decisions for everyone else, but they would try to encourage the broadest possible participation. The strike will succeed only because they are able to make it succeed—together. Therefore, you (the teacher) will play no role in their discussions. Once their strike meeting begins, you will be just an observer. It will be up to the entire class to decide how to make decisions and what those decisions should be.

4. Once they understand that you won't assist with their deliberations, you may want to discuss with them some of the ways they can reach decisions. For example, they could select a chairperson who would then call on individuals to speak and propose when votes might be taken. Perhaps they will want to avoid leaders entirely— students might raise hands, with the last person to speak calling on the next speaker and so on. Or a rotating chairperson might be chosen—one chair per question, for example. The teacher's job is merely to help the students to make their own decisions. This is an essential part of the role play.

5. Tell students that the questions in the handout were genuine concerns in the actual strike. (It's not important that students arrive at the historically accurate answers—they'll be able to find those answers in their homework reading. What is important is that they discuss the questions in terms of the IWW principles and goals.) Remind them to answer each of the questions as fully as possible. Tell them you will be available only if they have difficulty understanding any of the six questions.

6. Allow them to begin their meeting. Because students are not used to having to organize a discussion without the assistance of an authority figure, they may find it rough going at first. That's fine. Let them discover their own problems and solutions. Intervene only if you sense they are hopelessly frustrated, and then only to help them establish a clear decision-making process. As the meeting progresses, take notes on both their decision-making successes and failures and on the different ideas and arguments that students raise in answering the questions. I like to take verbatim notes on their deliberations and read portions of these back to students as a way to begin a following day of discussion.

7. At the conclusion of the strike meeting, ask students to write evaluations of their decisions and of the process that brought them to those decisions. Taking this break for reflection sometimes enables a class to discuss experiences a little more thoughtfully.

The Strike Continues, Reflection

1. Tell students that it's time to find out how the strikers actually solved the problems with which the class has been dealing. Tell them to listen closely to compare the real decisions with the ones they reached.

2. Read aloud or distribute to students, "Lawrence, 1912—Part 2."

3. Compare their decisions in the first problem-solving session to what actually happened as described in the reading.

4. Discuss students' decision-making process. There will be opportunity for a fuller discussion later in the lesson. At this point, simply raise:

   - What was good about how the class conducted the discussion?

   - What difficulties did you have? Why?

   - How might the organizational meeting have gone better? Try to reach some decisions here because the class will soon be in the same group decision-making process.

5. (Optional) Encourage students to produce either a strike leaflet directed toward individuals still crossing picket lines, or an appeal for aid to workers in other cities. In each case, the leaflet or appeal should urge support for the strike and offer suggestions for how others could help. Encourage students to be both eloquent and artistic in their appeals. You might suggest that students complete their "leaflets" in the form of songs. One year a number of students wrote and performed songs based on contemporary melodies they were familiar with. While not strictly historically accurate, these efforts added drama and spirit to the lesson.

6. Give students "Lawrence Problem-Solving #2." For homework or in class before beginning discussion, ask students to jot down ideas for each question in preparation for the discussion.

The Strike Continues, Part 2

1. Reconvene the class as an IWW planning meeting, exactly as with the first decision-making session. This time, the task is to discuss specific challenges faced by the IWW during the strike, described in "Lawrence Problem-Solving #2." Remind students of their dual goal: to win the strike and to build the union in line with IWW principles. Again, students address these questions without teacher direction. Clarify any misunderstandings of the questions on the problem-solving sheet and take notes on students' discussion.

2. At the conclusion of the discussion, distribute "Lawrence, 1912—Part 3," either as homework or to read aloud in class.

Concluding the Strike

1. Review the eight questions of "Lawrence Problem-Solving #2" one by one, asking students to compare their own decisions with what actually happened.

2. Tell the class that a year and a half after the strike, IWW membership in Lawrence plummeted from 14,000 to 700. Ask what might have caused the decline. Four factors are mentioned in the reading: decisions made by the IWW; government action; the effect produced by capitalist business cycles; and management strategy.

3. Ask whether the union could have acted differently to maintain its strength. (Rather than dispersing the most skilled organizers to other strikes or organizing drives, the union could have kept them in Lawrence, where they would be able to develop activities and services. The union might also have made efforts to organize all the mills in other locations owned by the same companies.)

4. Some other questions to raise about the strike:

   - Democracy is a key feature of what was called the Bread and Roses Strike. Are

Strikers held back by soldiers, Lawrence, Mass., 1912.

there groups that benefit from maintaining hierarchy and inequality? Who in Lawrence had a stake in inequality?

- What are the various ways that these groups can oppose workers? (Some possible answers: layoffs, moving production to places where workers aren't organized, police, passing laws, structuring the workplace to increase divisiveness.)

- What might workers in Lawrence have learned about "winning" a strike? Can "winning" mean something more than successfully securing higher wages? What changes in their own abilities or attitudes did workers "win"?

- What experiences did people in Lawrence have during the strike that allowed them to make significant changes in their lives? in their attitudes toward themselves? in their abilities to think and act effectively with others?—Note: This question aims to explore the idea that people undergo important changes when they are involved in a struggle for something they believe in. More than this, the specific character of the strike in Lawrence enhanced people's ability to change.

5. Discuss with students their decision-making process:

- Did your problem-solving improve from the first time to the second?

- The IWW valued workers making decisions themselves, without bosses or union officials telling them what to do. Based on your experience together, do you see why the IWW would think this process so important?

- As a class, what difficulties did you have in making decisions that a group of workers might also encounter?

- What kind of decision-making skills are taught as part of your education? Are you encouraged to work and think together without an authority figure leading you?

- If not, why isn't this skill taught more widely?

- Would any social groups feel threatened if high schools graduated students who were comfortable making decisions collectively and who expected to continue to operate that way in their work lives? ■

This activity is adapted from Bill Bigelow and Norm Diamond, The Power in Our Hands: A Curriculum on the History of Work and Workers in the United States *(Monthly Review Press, 1988).*

You Are in the IWW

THE YEAR IS 1912. New industries, based on new kinds of machinery, new ways of organizing work, and more use of unskilled and foreign-born workers, are flourishing. Most established labor unions (such as those in the American Federation of Labor, or AFL) have not tried to organize unskilled workers. But one has: the Industrial Workers of the World, the IWW. You are a member of this union.

You feel strongly that the IWW is the only union with a future because it understands what's really going on in this country. As you see it, the other major labor federation, the AFL, is living in the past. It's from a time when most work was done by craftsmen owning their own tools—each trade was difficult and required lots of skill and time to learn. When there was conflict between skilled workers and owners, the craftsmen formed trade unions to protect themselves. These were unions based on a particular craft—shoemakers, carpenters, bricklayers, and the like.

But times have changed. The hand tool has almost disappeared. Instead, there are huge factories with machines run by workers who don't own their own tools and have little control over how the work is performed. Ownership has also changed. Now, an individual factory may be only one of many controlled by the same owners. Yet the AFL craft unions continue as if nothing has changed—they still organize craft by craft. In your view, this divides workers and lets the owners play one craft or one factory against another. For instance, when workers in one factory go on strike,

the owners simply increase production elsewhere.

The IWW, on the other hand, believes in the idea of One Big Union. And you think that the IWW is right: all workers—skilled and unskilled, native-born and foreign-born, men and women—should be in the same union. In your mind, it's time to stop this nonsense of organizing only skilled, American-born men. You like what Big Bill Haywood—one of the most famous IWW members—says: "The AFL organizes like this"—separating his fingers as far apart as they can go, and naming the separate crafts. "The IWW organizes like this"—making a tight fist and shaking it at the bosses.

There are other important differences between the IWW and the AFL craft unions. The AFL wants just a little bigger piece of the pie. Higher wages, shorter hours, improved conditions—that's all the AFL is after. You IWW members see these goals as shortsighted. For you, working people's problems will only begin to be solved when workers take over all the workplaces and run them together for the benefit of everyone—not just for the private profit of the owners. As long as owners run industry for themselves, there will be continual conflict between them and the workers. You believe that all wealth is produced by the workers, so all wealth should be controlled by the workers—what do owners produce?

Thus, the IWW's goal is not only for higher wages or shorter hours, but also to improve the whole society. Workplaces and all of society should be run by the people who produce, the

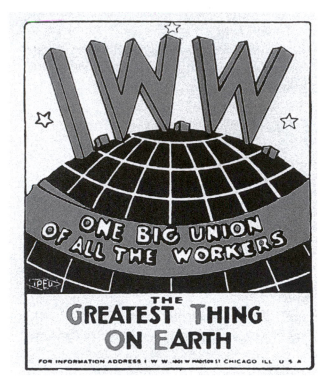

However, as you came to know the IWW people better, you saw they run their organization in a way that actually teaches people to be leaders and thinkers. The IWW halls have libraries. Workers hold classes to teach one another. They put on plays and sing together. Most importantly, the IWW also insists that all members participate in making decisions in the organization.

And the AFL seems to be afraid of strikes. The IWW isn't. What better learning experience could there be than a confrontation between capitalists and workers? A strike allows the IWW to show workers that, "The capitalist class and the working class have nothing in common." Strikes are an important chance for workers to learn that they can trust each other and make decisions together.

The IWW is more than an organization, it's a social movement. One of the slogans of the IWW is, "We must form the structure of the new society in the shell of the old."

You in the IWW don't believe in the idea of "follow the leader." Your goal is for every union member to be a "leader." ■

people who do the work.

At first when you heard IWW members talking like this you thought it was a little silly. "They're dreaming," you said to yourself. "What do workers know about running anything?"

You Are in the IWW: Membership Questions

1. As an IWW member, what do you think are the most important differences between the IWW and the AFL? (List these on a separate sheet of paper.)

2. Write an "interior monologue" imagining some of the life experiences that led you to join the IWW. Where are you from? What is your work experience? What attracted you to the IWW? What worries do you have? What hopes do you have? Write this in the first person.

Lawrence, 1912—Part 1
The Strike Is On!

WORK CONDITIONS IN LAWRENCE, Massachusetts, were undergoing the same kinds of changes occurring in industries across the United States. In the 1880s, the mill owners brought in new machinery and lowered wages. They began to recruit immigrants from Europe. At first, they brought in just one nationality; then, to keep the workforce divided, another and another. To make the work seem attractive, they sent postcards to different parts of Europe that showed workers leaving the mills carrying bags of money on their way to the bank.

By 1912, there were dozens of different ethnic groups in Lawrence, speaking almost 30 different languages: Italian and Polish, Ukrainian and Yiddish, Portuguese and French. This Massachusetts city now produced more cloth than any other city in the country. And yet workers often couldn't afford to buy jackets. Malnutrition was common. Housing was crowded and lacked light and sanitation. Life expectancy of a Lawrence *worker* was 22 years less than that of a factory *owner*. Because of low wages, entire families had to work in the mills. Of the more than 30,000 workers, half were teenagers. In fact, one half of the children in Lawrence between 14 and 18 years old worked in the mills. A small percentage of the workers had better paid, skilled jobs. The AFL craft union had 208 members. It did not have a contract with the owners.

Not one mill owner lived in Lawrence. Profits were rising, and the pace of work was continually increasing. In 1905, the owners decided that each worker in the woolen mills would operate two looms instead of one. In the cotton mills, every worker now tended twelve different machines at once.

Supervisors pressured women workers for dates and to provide sexual favors. They were abusive and disrespectful to foreign-born workers. Water in the mills was so contaminated by the heat and dust that it was undrinkable. Supervisors sold bottled water at a profit. The company paid part of workers' wages on what was called the "premium system." This meant that any worker who was sick for more than one day a month, or failed to produce the amount set by the supervisor (because his or her machine broke, for instance), lost the premium. Since skilled workers received their premium according to the production of the unskilled workers under them, they also pressured unskilled workers and played favorites.

The usual work week was 56 hours. Concerned about health conditions, the state legislature passed a law limiting work hours for children and women to 54 hours (six days a week, nine hours a day). Immediately, the owners saw a way to take advantage of this reform. They sped up the work yet again, so that the same amount of cloth was produced in 54 hours as had been produced in 56.

Now the question was: would the workers' pay be lowered? Since housing costs weren't going down, any pay cut would simply mean less to eat. On January 12, workers opened their pay envelopes to find ... a pay cut.

After a few stunned seconds, in desperation, someone yelled, "Strike!"

Winslow Homer sketched Lawrence, Mass. workers as they left the textile mills at the end of the day. This appeared in Harper's Weekly, *July 25, 1868.*

The strike spread quickly. Within days, more than 20,000 workers were picketing, often singing as they marched.

The national president of the AFL union came to Lawrence to try to discourage the strike. He was even more harsh than management in criticizing the strikers. His members—generally American-born skilled workers—crossed picket lines and continued to work. The union president's tactic was to show his loyalty to management in hopes of being rewarded with union recognition. He offered mill owners a deal: sign a contract with his union and the AFL would continue to oppose the strike. Confident of victory, and opposing unions in any form, the owners refused.

After about three weeks, the strike was so effective that there remained little work for the skilled workers. Then they too joined the strike. Thousands of strikers became members of the Industrial Workers of the World—the IWW. ■

Lawrence Problem-Solving #1
Getting Organized

1. There are a number of different mills in Lawrence on strike. This involves over 30,000 workers. Many different ethnic groups are represented in Lawrence. Lots of different languages are spoken and there are a number of cultures in the city.

   Question: How is the strike going to be "led"? Who will decide how to negotiate, what the demands of the strike should be, what tactics to use, whether to end the strike, etc.?

2. Many of the workers in Lawrence are illiterate. People speak a number of different languages. There are thousands of people involved in the strike, in more than one factory.

   Question: Specifically, what kind of "organizational structure" should we use throughout the strike? (Some possibilities: large meetings involving all the strikers, elected representatives, rotating leadership, some other method.)

3. **Question: How should any meetings we hold be run? By whom?**

4. **Question: How can we make sure that we keep the strikers unified?**

5. With the thugs hired by management, the picket line can be dangerous and some people feel that it is no place for a woman. These workers point out that women are not even allowed to vote in national or local elections. Remember, the year is 1912.

   Question: Should women be allowed to participate in the strike? If so, in what capacity?

6. There have been charges in the newspapers that some of the strikers are "illegal immigrants" who came to this country only in order to send money home.

   Question: What should we do about these people?

Lawrence, 1912—Part 2
Unity in Diversity

AN OUTDOOR MEETING of thousands of strikers—men, women, and children—discussed and then agreed on the demands of the strike. People would not return to work until four conditions were met:

1. A wage increase

2. Extra pay for working overtime

3. An end to the premium system of payment and the pressures it brought

4. No penalties or discrimination against strikers

Each day, there were mass meetings organized according to nationality—Hungarians met with Hungarians, Italians with Italians, etc. These were the major decision-making meetings, chaired by people elected from the group. Here delegates reported to the strikers and received further directions from them.

A strike committee met every morning to coordinate activities. It consisted of elected delegates, four from each of 14 nationality groups, 56 in all, covering every workplace and every type of job. Delegates could be replaced at any time by the group that elected them. A second committee of 56 served as a back-up in case members of the strike committee were arrested. Delegates met outdoors so that their discussions could be heard and evaluated by everyone. In these gatherings the many strikers who attended could gain a renewed sense of their own numbers and strength.

On Saturdays and Sundays, huge meetings brought everyone together, tens of thousands of strikers and their families. At these and at the daily ethnic group meetings, there was entertainment, in addition to reports and discussions. People sang together, danced, and enjoyed performances by their neighbors.

These were meetings for all strikers, whether or not they were IWW members. In addition, the IWW called special meetings for women and children to encourage their participation and leadership. Organizers talked extensively with husbands to overcome their resistance to wives speaking in public or marching on the picket lines. In the difficult conditions of the strike, people discovered many new abilities: chairing meetings, speaking in public, organizing committees.

There were numerous efforts to divide the strikers. Newspapers and some religious leaders criticized husbands for permitting their wives and daughters to play an active role. Attempts were made to pit ethnic groups against each other. Some priests told Irish workers, for instance, that they were superior to the non-English-speaking nationalities. City officials charged that some workers were "illegal immigrants" and should be deported. These efforts took their toll. Some husbands kept their wives at home. Some nationalities participated more actively than did others. Overwhelmingly, however, the strikers remained firm, maintaining a belief that everyone had a right to work in decent conditions and to develop fully his or her capabilities. ■

Lawrence Problem-Solving #2
Can We Win?

1. Early in the strike, without meeting with any of the strikers, the employers agree to restore the 56-hour pay rate. If we don't go back to work, they may withdraw that decision.

   Question: Shall we claim victory and go back to work? If not, what should we do?

2. The commanding officer of the militia who has been sent to Lawrence insists that different groups of strikers should meet separately with each employer. His hope is that agreements will be reached with some employers and that some strikers will return to work.

   Question: How do we respond?

3. Our strike committee has just traveled to Boston to meet with the president of the largest group of mills. No agreement was reached. But now false reports are being circulated and newspapers are announcing that a settlement was reached and that the strike is over. Tomorrow is Monday. We know that employers are gearing up to reopen the mills. If people believe the rumors and return to work, the strike will be lost.

   Question: What can we do?

4. There are still some people crossing the picket lines. Some of them are showing up at the relief committees while continuing to work.

   Question: Should we feed them?

5. Violence has been increasing. Two people have been killed. A policeman shot a woman as she was picketing. A boy was bayoneted in the back while fleeing the militia. Our people are scared. Some want to end the violence by returning to work. Others are becoming restless and want to fight back with violence.

   Question: What should we tell both groups?

6. Because of the violence, some of us fear for the safety of our children. Not only that, our resources here are limited and the children are hungrier than usual. Having members from so many different backgrounds means we can learn from each other's experiences and traditions. One group has said that during a bitter strike in their country, children are sometimes sent to the homes of workers in other cities. We have many supporters in New York City and elsewhere.

   Question: Is this something we should do? If we send the children, is there some way they can win even greater support for our strike?

7. Martial law has been declared. All picketing is now against the law, as is any gathering of more than two people on the street.

   Question: How can we respond? (Without picketing and meeting, our strike will die.)

8. A "Citizens Association" has been formed by local merchants and city officials against "outside agitators." "After all," they say, "our own good Lawrence folk wouldn't dream of striking." The mayor has launched a "God and Country" campaign. Businesses are flying American flags, citizens are being encouraged to wear patriotic lapel pins, all directed against the IWW. We too love the country, but we have a different vision of what it should become. We also now have 14,000 members in Lawrence.

   Question: How can we respond?

Lawrence, 1912—Part 3
The Outcome

Pressures and Response

Not long after the strikers agreed on all four demands, the employers posted notices that they were restoring the former wages. For 54 hours' work (but 56 hours worth of production because of speedup), workers were to receive the same amount they had been paid for working 56 hours. If a significant number accepted this offer and returned to the mills, the strike would have been broken. Clearly the employers were trying to undermine worker solidarity.

Many workers must have been tempted. They were not used to challenging authority. Living conditions on strike were difficult. However, people remembered that living conditions had also been difficult when they were working. The strike meetings and activities were beginning to give them a sense of their own strength and hope for a better settlement. The strikers held firm.

There were other efforts to divide the strikers. Employers agreed to negotiate, but only on a company-by-company basis, not with the strike committee representing all the strikers. Recognizing that separate negotiations or even settlements would pull them apart, the strikers refused. An agency of the Massachusetts government intervened. The strike committee agreed to let the agency try to get the employers to sit down with the strikers and negotiate (that is, to *mediate*). However, the committee refused to let the agency decide the agenda or what the settlement would be (that is, to *arbitrate*).

The strikers fell into a trap. The president of the largest textile company agreed to meet in Boston with strike committee representatives. The meeting took place over a weekend and did not lead to an agreement. As strike committee members returned to Lawrence on Sunday, they found that false rumors were being spread, along with newspaper stories, that a settlement had been reached. Supervisors were already gearing up the mills for the next day. The strike committee decided on a rally for early Monday morning. From the rally, thousands of strikers marched in a huge parade, stopping and alerting people who had believed the false reports.

Both employers and government continued pressure. Martial law was declared. Twenty-two companies of militia took over the town, including many Harvard boys carrying bayonets "up to teach those workers a lesson." Any gathering of more than two people on the streets was banned, as was the stationing of pickets near the mills.

Strike Tactics

Their use of a parade led the workers on strike to other new tactics. Since the merchants couldn't survive if the order against gathering was enforced downtown, the strikers responded by going to the business district first. They formed large groups, posing as customers, milling in and out of stores but buying nothing. Other customers, of course, were reluctant to shop. The merchants quickly insisted that the authorities withdraw their order against gathering. Then the strikers formed an "endless chain of pickets," 7,000 to 10,000 people, circling the entire industrial district. They maintained this constantly moving picket line for the remaining weeks of the strike.

Keeping up morale was the key to maintaining the strike, so providing for the needs of strikers and their families was an important task of the strikers' organizations. Publicity and finance committees got support from workers all across the country. Relief committees, organized by nationality, distributed food or money for food and fuel to more than 50,000 of the 86,000 people who lived in Lawrence. Some of the people still working tried to sneak in line and get assistance. They were always encouraged to stop crossing the picket lines, but were refused relief if they didn't join the strike. The AFL set up its own relief organization, providing aid only to people who agreed to end their strike.

BAR SHIPMENT OF STRIKE CHILDREN; WOMEN CLUBBED

Youngsters Trampled in Riot When Lawrence Police Halt Exportation.

MOTHERS FIGHT WITH TEETH AND HATPINS

Violence

With so many workers away from their jobs, the authorities continually claimed the strikers threatened violence. As workers left their looms the first day, the municipal government rang the city hall bells in a riot alarm. When workers first began picketing outside the mills, company supervisors on the rooftops sprayed them with icy water. When drenched and freezing workers retaliated by throwing pieces of ice, the police moved in. Those strikers who were caught received ten-minute trials and sentences of a year in jail.

When they left their looms, some strikers had cut the belts that transmitted power. During the strike, when some workers continued to cross picket lines, the strikers tried persuasion, pressure, and even intimidation. Years of pent-up frustration could have led to disorganized fighting or further attacks on property. Instead, the strikers almost always honored the IWW call for discipline and peaceful protest.

There were many provocations. Police raids uncovered dynamite, and newspapers across the country blamed the strikers. Police used this episode as an excuse to close the industrial district to pickets and to harass workers in other ways. A trial showed that a small group of local merchants had planted the dynamite to discredit the strikers, then called the police. The conspiracy was planned in textile company offices.

A woman picketer was shot and killed. In spite of many witnesses who identified a particular policeman as the killer, police arrested two IWW leaders, Arturo Giovannitti and Joseph Ettor, who had been speaking three miles away. That morning, streetcars were stopped and their windows smashed. Strikers identified thugs, hired by the mill owners, as responsible. Police repeatedly attacked picket lines, beating people so severely that pregnant women miscarried. A boy, fleeing the militia, was bayoneted in the back and died.

Because of difficult conditions, the violence, and the shortage of food and fuel, the strikers decided to accept another form of aid. As an expression of solidarity, workers in New York and Philadelphia invited young children of the strikers to come stay with them. The first trainloads of young people were welcomed warmly and also created favorable publicity for the strike. The next time parents took a group of children to the train station in Lawrence, police surrounded the station, then attacked, severely beating both children and parents. Police separated children and parents and took them to jail. The authorities began proceedings to permanently take the children from their parents.

Victory

Ultimately, the authorities' use of violence backfired, and the strikers' discipline prevailed. With families waiting in other cities to receive the children, the train station brutality became international news. A Socialist Party representative began Congressional hearings about the situation in Lawrence. The hearings focused not only on the immediate violence, but on the long-term violence of hunger, inadequate clothing and housing, early deaths, and the stunted lives of children.

By now the strike had gone on for more than two months. The companies kept the machinery running to make it sound as if work continued, although in fact they had not been able to produce any textiles. More than most industries, textile companies were vulnerable to public outrage and Congressional pressure. Their high profits were based in part on a tariff that kept out foreign textiles and gave the U.S. industry a near-monopoly. Now public anger at textile owners could lead Congress to end the tariff. Management decided to settle the strike. They asked the strike committee to begin serious negotiations and quickly agreed to all four of the strikers' demands.

A meeting of 15,000 strikers voted to accept the agreement. There would be wage increases, with the greatest increases going to the workers who had been most poorly paid. There would be extra pay for overtime work. No worker would be discriminated against for having been on strike. The premium system would be changed to reduce the pressure, with payment every two weeks instead of once a month.

Strikers returned to work; children came home to their families. The IWW, tiny before the strike, now had 14,000 members in Lawrence. And the struggle continued. The mayor began a "God and Country" campaign, using patriotism to claim the IWW was "un-American." IWW members threatened a boycott of "God and Country" merchants, and merchants ended their campaign. The two IWW leaders, Ettor and Giovannitti, remained in jail on trumped-up murder charges. The IWW declared a political strike in Lawrence. Thousands of workers stayed away from work for a day to protest the continued jailing and to insist on a fair trial. Textile workers in other cities also threatened to strike if the two men were framed. The textile companies fired 1,500 workers for participating in the political strike. However, when the IWW threatened renewed strike action, owners backed down completely, rehiring every worker. A jury trial found the IWW leaders not guilty.

Postscript

The Lawrence strikers won a victory that most of the organized labor movement had thought impossible. They united women and men, mainly unskilled workers from dozens of nationality groups. They vastly increased their own self-confidence, skills, and knowledge, and built what seemed to be a powerful local union. Yet within the next few years, the union was again reduced to a small group and management succeeded in taking back some of the strikers' gains.

The reasons for this decline are complex. Some of the IWW's most skilled organizers left Lawrence after the strike, to spread the victory and try to build unions elsewhere. There was increased repression nationally against the IWW, with more trials, deportations, and even massacres of supporters. The more important cause, however, was probably the national economy and how management took advantage of that. In times of recession over the next few years, owners laid off workers who had been especially active in the union. They also lowered wages and sped up working conditions. Further, the companies expanded to locations where workers were not organized. Now they could outlast a strike in one location by increasing production in their mills elsewhere.

In the new large-scale industries, militant workers in just one location would have limited strength. Factory- and citywide organizing efforts were not enough; the next step would require workers to organize in whole industries. Until that happened, indeed long after, the "singing strike" continued to provide inspiration. ■

Questions

1. What are the important similarities between the answers you came up with in class and what the strikers actually decided in Lawrence? What are the important differences?

2. Why do you suppose the IWW lost so many members in Lawrence in the few years after the strike? Could they have done anything differently to preserve and strengthen their influence?

3. From your problem-solving in class, what have you learned about making decisions in groups? For example, why is it so difficult for people to make decisions together? Why don't school systems place a higher priority on teaching these skills? What are good methods of solving problems as a group?

4. What are some of the "lessons" for us today from the Lawrence strike?

Rethinking the Teaching of the Vietnam War

THE UNITED NATIONS HAS DECLARED this the Decade of Peace. The troubling irony is that teaching for peace must begin with a study of war. Unless we look carefully at the dynamics of war and come to grips with the root causes of global conflicts, we have no way to convincingly propose solutions—no way to imagine peace.

Sadly, when it comes to probing the root causes of the Vietnam War, not a single major U.S. history text glances back beyond the 1950s. Why was the U.S. involved in Vietnam? As James Loewen points out in *Lies My Teacher Told Me*, his critique of 12 best-selling high school history texts, "Most textbooks simply dodge the issue. Here is a representative analysis, from *American Adventures*: 'Later in the 1950s, war broke out in South Vietnam. This time the United States gave aid to the South Vietnamese government.' 'War broke out'—what could be simpler!"

The textbooks mirror the amnesia of U.S. policy makers. There is a startling encounter in the Vietnam War documentary *Hearts and Minds* between producer Peter Davis and Walt Rostow, former adviser to President Johnson. Davis wants Rostow to talk about why the United States got involved in Vietnam. Rostow is incredulous: "Are you really asking me this goddamn silly question?" That's "pretty pedestrian stuff," he complains. But Rostow finally answers: "The problem began in its present phase after the Sputnik, the launching of Sputnik, in 1957, October."

> *Students need to learn to distinguish explanations from descriptions, like "war broke out," or "chaos erupted."*

Sputnik? 1957? At one blow, the former adviser erases years of history to imply that somehow the Soviet Union was behind it all.

The "present phase" caveat notwithstanding, Rostow ignores the World War II cooperation between the United States and the Viet Minh; Ho Chi Minh's repeated requests that the U.S. acknowledge Vietnamese sovereignty; the U.S. refusal to recognize the 1945 Declaration of Independence of the Democratic Republic of Vietnam; $2 billion in U.S. military support for the restoration of French domination, including the near-use of nuclear weapons during the decisive battle of Dien Bien Phu, according to the Army's own history of the war; and the well-documented U.S. subversion of the 1954 Geneva peace accords. All occurred before the launching of Sputnik.

When teachers pattern our curricula after these kinds of nonexplanatory explanations, we mystify the origins not just of the war in Vietnam, but of everything we teach. Students need to learn to distinguish explanations from descriptions, like "war broke out," or "chaos erupted." Thinking about social events as having concrete causes, constantly asking "Why?" and "In whose interests?" need to become critical habits of the mind for us and for our students. It's only through developing the tools of deep questioning that students can attempt to make sense of today's global conflicts. However, especially when teaching complicated events like the war in Vietnam, bypassing explanation in favor of description can be seductive. After all, there's so much *stuff* about the war in Vietnam: so many films; so many novels, short stories, and poetry; so many veterans who can come in and speak to the class. These are all vital resources, but unless built on a foundation of causes for the war, using these can be more voyeuristic than educational.

Roots of a War

A video I've found useful in prompting students to explore a bit of the history of Vietnam and the sources of U.S. involvement is the first episode of the PBS presentation *Vietnam: A Television History* [available in many libraries]. Called "Roots of a War," it offers an overview of Vietnamese resistance to French colonialism (which began in the mid-19th century) and to the Japanese occupation during World War II. My students find the video a bit dry, so in order for students not to feel overwhelmed by information, I pause it often to talk about key incidents and issues. Some of the images are powerful: Vietnamese men carrying white-clad Frenchmen on their backs, and French picture-postcards of the severed heads of Vietnamese resisters —cards that troops sent home to sweethearts in Paris, as the narrator tells us, inscribed, "With kisses from Hanoi." The goal of French colonialism is presented truthfully and starkly: "To transform Vietnam into a source of profit." The narrator explains, "Exports of rice stayed high even if it meant the peasants starved." Significantly, many of those who tell the story of colonialism and the struggle against it are Vietnamese. Instead of the nameless generic peasants of so many Hollywood Vietnam War

AP Images

Ho Chi Minh, right, became president of the Democratic Republic of Vietnam. Vo Nguyen Giap, left, was Minister of the Interior.

movies, here, at least in part, Vietnamese get to tell their own stories.

Toward the end of the episode, Dr. Tran Duy Hung recounts the Vietnamese independence celebration in Hanoi's Ba Dinh Square following the Japanese defeat—and occurring on the very day of the formal Japanese surrender aboard the USS Missouri in Tokyo Bay, September 2, 1945: "I can say that the most moving moment was when President Ho Chi Minh climbed the steps, and the national anthem was sung. It was the first time that the national anthem of Vietnam was sung in an official ceremony. Uncle Ho then read the Declaration of Independence, which was a short document. As he was reading, Uncle Ho stopped and asked, 'Compatriots, can you hear me?' This simple question went into the hearts of everyone there. After a moment of silence, they all shouted, 'Yes, we hear you.' And I can say that we did not just shout with our mouths, but with all our hearts. The hearts of over 400,000 people standing in the square then."

Dr. Hung recalls that moments later, a small plane began circling overhead and swooped down over the crowd. When people recognized the stars and stripes of the U.S. flag, they cheered enthusiastically, believing its presence to be a kind of independence ratification. The image of the 1945 crowd in northern Vietnam applauding a U.S. military aircraft offers a poignant reminder of historical could-have-beens.

Although this is not the episode's conclusion, I stop the video at this point. How will the U.S. government respond? Will it recognize an independent Vietnam or stand by as France attempts to reconquer its lost colony? Will the United States even aid France in this effort? This is a choice-point that would influence the course of human history, and through role play I want to bring it to life in the classroom. Of course, I could simply tell them what happened, or give them materials to read. But a role play that brings to life the perspectives of key social groups, allows students to experience, rather than just hear about, aspects of this historical crossroads. As prelude, we read the Vietnamese Declaration of Independence, available in the fine collection, *Vietnam and America: A Documented History*, edited by Marvin Gettleman, Jane Franklin, Marilyn Young, and H. Bruce Franklin [New York: Grove Press, 1985], as well as in *Vietnam: A History in Documents*, edited by Gareth Porter [New York: New American Library, 1981].

Role-Playing a Historic Choice

I include here the two core roles of the role play: members of the Viet Minh and French government/business leaders. In teaching this period, I sometimes include other roles: U.S. corporate executives, labor activists, farmers, and British government officials deeply worried about their own colonial interests, as well as Vietnamese landlords allied with the French—this last, to reflect the class as well as anticolonial dimension of the Vietnamese independence movement.

Each group has been invited to a meeting with President Harry S. Truman—which, as students learn later, never took place—to present its position on the question of Vietnamese independence. I portray President Truman and chair the meeting. Members of each group must explain:

- How they were affected by World War II;

- Why the United States should care what happens in Vietnam, along with any responsibilities the U.S. might have (and in the case of the French, why the United States should care what happens in France);

- Whether the United States should feel threatened by communism in Vietnam, or in the case of the French leaders, France;

- What they want President Truman to do about the Vietnamese Declaration of Independence—support it, ignore it, oppose it;

- And whether the United States government should grant loans to the French, and if it supports loans, what strings should be attached.

Obviously, the more knowledge students have about pre-1945 Vietnam, France, and World War II in general, as well as the principles of communism, the more sophisticated treatment they'll be able to give to their roles. [An excellent film on U.S. Communism is *Seeing Red*, produced by Jim Klein and Julia Reichert, available from New Day Films, and can be helpful.] However, even without a thorough backgrounding, the lesson works well to introduce the main issues in this important historical choice-point.

As in other role plays, to work students into their roles, I may ask them to create an individual persona by writing an interior monologue—one's inner thoughts—on their post-war hopes and fears. Students can read these to a partner, or share them in a small group.

In the meeting/debate, students-as-Viet Minh argue on behalf of national independence. They may remind Truman of the help that the Viet Minh gave to the Allies during World War II, denounce French colonialism, and recall the United States' own history in throwing off European colonialism.

The students-as-French counter that the would-be Vietnamese rulers are communists and therefore a threat to world peace. Like the Vietnamese, the French remind Truman that they too were World War II allies and are now in need of a helping hand. In order to revive a prosperous and capitalist France, they need access to the resources of Vietnam. Because the United States has an interest in a stable Europe, one that is non-communist and open for investment, they should support French efforts to regain control of Vietnam.

I play a cranky Truman, and poke at inconsistencies in students' arguments. I especially prod each side to question and criticize the other directly. [For suggestions on conducting a role play, see "Role Plays: Show, Don't Tell," in the Rethinking Schools publication *Rethinking Our*

Classrooms: Teaching for Equity and Justice, Vol. 1, pp. 130-132.]

The structure of the meeting itself alerts students to the enormous power wielded by the United States government at the end of World War II, and that the government was maneuvering on a global playing field.

As students come to see, U.S. policy makers did not decide the Vietnam question solely, if at all, on issues of morality, or even on issues related directly to Vietnam. As historian Gabriel Kolko writes in *The Roots of American Foreign Policy,* "even in 1945 the United States regarded Indo-China almost exclusively as the object of Great Power diplomacy and conflict. ... [A]t no time did the desires of the Vietnamese themselves assume a role in the shaping of United States policy."

Following the whole-group debate, we shed our roles to debrief. I ask: What were some of the points brought out in discussion that you agreed

A role play that brings to life the perspectives of key social groups, allows students to experience, rather than just hear about, aspects of this historical crossroads.

with? Do you think Truman ever met with Vietnamese representatives? What would a U.S. president take into account in making a decision like this? What did Truman decide? Which powerful groups might seek to influence Vietnam policy? How should an important foreign policy question like this one be decided?

To discover what Truman did and why, we study a timeline drawn from a number of books on Vietnam, including the one by Kolko mentioned above, his *Anatomy of a War* [Pantheon, 1985], Marilyn Young's *The Vietnam Wars: 1945-1990* [HarperCollins, 1991], *The Pentagon Papers* [Bantam, 1971], as well as excerpts from Chapter 18 of Howard Zinn's *A People's History of the United States* [HarperCollins, 2003]. It's a complicated history involving not only the French and Vietnamese, but also Chiang Kai-shek's nationalist Chinese forces, the British, and the Japanese. What becomes clear is that at the close of World War II,

Marine commando forces of the U.S.-supported French Expeditionary Corps land in Vietnam on July 27, 1950.

the United States was in a position to end almost 100 years of French domination in Vietnam. The French government was desperate for U.S. aid and would not have defied an American decision to support Vietnamese independence. Nevertheless, U.S. leaders chose a different route, ultimately contributing about $2 billion to the French effort to reconquer Vietnam.

While a separate set of decisions led to the commitment of U.S. troops in Vietnam, the trajectory was set in the period just after World War II. The insights students glean from this role play inform our study of Vietnam throughout the unit. Along with the timeline, just mentioned, which traces U.S. economic and military aid to France, we follow up with a point-by-point study of the 1954 Geneva agreement ending the war between the French and Vietnamese; and from the perspective of peasants and plantation laborers in southern Vietnam, students evaluate the 1960 revolutionary platform of the National Liberation Front. Students later read a number of quotations from scholars and politicians offering opinions on why we fought in Vietnam. Presidents Kennedy, Johnson, and Nixon assert in almost identical language that the United States was safeguarding freedom and democracy in South Vietnam. President Kennedy: "For the last decade we have been helping the South Vietnamese to maintain their independence." Johnson: "We want nothing for ourselves—only that the people of South Vietnam be allowed to guide their own country in their own way." Students ponder these platitudes: If it were truly interested in Vietnam's "independence," why did the U.S. government support French colonialism?

On April 7, 1965, President Johnson gave a major policy speech on Vietnam at Johns Hopkins University. Here Johnson offered a detailed explanation for why the United States

Viet Minh and French officer in Hanoi, October 12, 1954. Following the Geneva Accords, the French withdrew from Vietnam.

was fighting in Vietnam [included in *The Viet-Nam Reader*, edited by Marcus Raskin and Bernard Fall, pp. 343-350]. Embedded in the speech was his version of the origins of the war. As Johnson, I deliver large portions of the speech, and students as truth-seeking reporters pepper me with critical questions and arguments drawn from the role play and other readings and activities. Following this session, they write a critique of LBJ's speech. Afterwards, we evaluate how several newspapers and journals—*The New York Times, The Oregonian, I.F. Stone's Weekly*—actually covered President Johnson's address.

None of the above is meant to suggest the outlines of a comprehensive curriculum on the Vietnam war. Here, I've concentrated on the need for engaging students in making explanations for the origins of U.S. government policy toward Vietnam. But policy choices had intimate implications for many people's lives, and through novels, short stories, poetry, interviews, and their own imaginations, students need also to explore the personal dimensions of diplomacy and political economy. And no study of the war would be complete without examining the dynamics of the massive movement to end that war. [The best film for this is *Sir! No Sir!*, available from www.teachingforchange.org, which looks at the antiwar movement within the U.S. military.] Especially when confronted with the horrifying images of slaughtered children in a film like *Remember My Lai*, the chilling sobs of a young Vietnamese boy whose father has been killed, in *Hearts and Minds*, or the anguish of American and Vietnamese women in *Regret to Inform*, our students need to know that millions of people tried to put a stop to the suffering—including U.S. soldiers themselves. And students should be encouraged to reflect deeply on which strategies for peace were most effective. Howard Zinn movingly describes this widespread opposition to the war in Chapter 18 of *A People's History of the United States*.

Indeed there is an entire history of resistance to which students have been denied access. For example, let them read the brilliant critique of the war that Dr. Martin Luther King, Jr. gave at Riverside Church, on April 4, 1967, exactly a year before his death:

> *What do the [Vietnamese] peasants think as we ally ourselves with the landlords and as we refuse to put any action into our many words concerning land reform? What do they think as we test out our latest weapons on them, just as the Germans tested out new medicine and new tortures in the concentration camps of Europe? Where are the roots of the independent Vietnam we claim to be building? Is it among these voiceless ones?*

Or let students listen to similar thoughts expressed more caustically in Bob Dylan's "Masters of War," or more satirically in Country Joe and the Fish's "Feel Like I'm Fixin' to Die Rag."

If we take the advice of the Walt Rostows and the textbook writers, and begin our study of the Vietnam war in the late 1950s, it's impossible to think intelligently about the U.S. role. The presidents said we were protecting the independence of "South Vietnam." Students need to travel back at least as far as 1945 to think critically about the invention of the country of South Vietnam that was intended to justify its "protection." The tens of thousands of U.S. deaths and the millions of Vietnamese deaths, along with the social and ecological devastation of Indochina require the harsh light of history to be viewed clearly.

If we are to give peace a chance, then we must think honestly about the roots of war. ■

Citizens of Hanoi, Vietnam, at a victory parade in October of 1954, after peace talks at Geneva led to the withdrawal of French colonial forces from all of Indochina. The United States had supported the French during the war.

French Business/ Government Leader

Time: Fall/Winter, 1945-46

YOU ARE A FRENCH BUSINESS EXECUTIVE and high-ranking government leader. Times are very difficult in France. During World War II, thousands of your people were killed, many factories were destroyed, crops burned, and animals killed. This has left your economy almost in ruins.

Because of hard times, many workers and poor people have turned to the Communists. The Communist Party is now the largest political party in France. An important reason the Communists are so popular is because they played a leading role in the resistance to the Nazis. You believe that, ultimately, the Communists want to take over the property of the wealthy and have all factories run by the government. The French Communist Party denies this, but you don't believe them.

As you see it, unless the economy quickly gets better, the Communists will be elected to control the government. But how to rebuild the economy?

Before World War II, France had a number of colonies around the world, the most important in Indochina, which includes the country of Vietnam. France got most of its rubber from Vietnam—also much coal, tin, and tungsten.

French businesses owned plantations and made great profits selling rice to other countries in Asia. Your government also forced the Vietnamese to buy certain French products, such as Bordeaux wine, so French companies made profits that way as well.

But here's your problem. During the war, the Japanese took control of Vietnam. The Vietnamese Communist leader, Ho Chi Minh, organized an army, the Viet Minh, to fight against the Japanese occupation. With Japan now defeated, the Viet Minh have declared Vietnam an independent country. However, as far as you are concerned, Vietnam is still French.

You are angry. The Viet Minh have already given some of the French-owned land to Vietnamese poor people—peasants. They have said that the wealth of Vietnam will now belong only to the Vietnamese.

If you can't take back your colony in Vietnam, French businesses will suffer tremendously. However, you don't have enough money to pay for a war against Ho Chi Minh. You need the support of a more powerful country to win back Vietnam from the Communists. The most powerful country in the world is the United States.

You also need the help of a stronger country to rebuild the cities, towns, and industries of France. You need loans and grants to buy American machinery and farm products like wheat and corn so you can get back on your feet. Remember, too, that if your economy doesn't begin to get stronger, the French Communists will probably win elections by offering the poor and workers some of the wealth of the rich.

But the United States needs you, too. They want to sell their extra products to you and to invest their extra money in French businesses. You might point out to the American president that, if the Communists come to power, they won't allow U.S. corporations to invest freely and take their profits back home. ■

Viet Minh Member

Time: Fall/Winter, 1945-46

YOU ARE A MEMBER OF THE VIET MINH and a supporter of the Democratic Republic of Vietnam. This is the first all-Vietnamese government in almost a hundred years—since the French first took over your country.

You are from a peasant family in Vietnam. You grew up hating the French colonialists who controlled your country. The French say they brought "civilization" to Vietnam, but in your eyes they brought nothing but misery.

In order to force the Vietnamese to work for them, the French put taxes on all "huts," as they called them, and on salt—an important ingredient in the Vietnamese diet. The only way you could get money to pay the hated taxes was to go to work for the French—on their railroads, in their mines, on their plantations. Conditions were hard. Many people died of injuries or diseases.

The French drafted your people to fight in their wars against other countries. Of course, you had no vote. The French provided few services; in Vietnam, they built more jails than schools and hospitals combined.

The French made fun of your music, your art, your religion. They even outlawed your village's homemade rice wine and forced you to buy their stronger French wine. The French also required each village to purchase a certain amount of opium.

Angered by all these injustices, you joined Ho Chi Minh's Viet Minh, an organization fighting for the independence of Vietnam. Like Ho Chi Minh, you became a Communist, believing that everyone should share the wealth of Vietnam, not just a few foreigners and the rich Vietnamese landlords who do their dirty work.

In 1940, the Japanese invaded Vietnam and you switched from fighting the French to fighting the Japanese. During the war you helped the United States, providing them valuable information and rescuing pilots who had been shot down.

When the Japanese were defeated, the Viet Minh took control of the country and proclaimed independence. This independence has begun to make a real difference in many people's lives. For the first time in Vietnam's history, national elections were held. People could choose their own leaders, Communist or non-Communist.

A literacy program was launched that some say taught as many as two and a half million people to read and write. The Viet Minh took over much of the land that the French had stolen and gave it back to the peasants. The new government passed a law legalizing labor unions and strikes and proclaiming an eight-hour workday.

Your goal is freedom and independence for your country. But the French appear to want to take back Vietnam. They complain about Communists like Ho Chi Minh. You will fight to the death before your country is made a colony again. You hope the United States government will support you in this freedom struggle. ■

A School Year Like No Other

Eyes on the Prize: "Fighting Back: 1957-1962"

"A SCHOOL YEAR LIKE NO OTHER." That's the narrator's understated description of the 1957-58 school year at Central High School in Little Rock, Ark., in the dramatic episode, "Fighting Back: 1957-1962," in the PBS *Eyes on the Prize* series.

More than 50 years after heavily armed federal troops escorted nine African American students into Central High School, it's easy to scoff at the results of desegregation. So black children can go to public schools formerly reserved for whites. So what? Is life within integrated schools equitably structured? Has desegregation significantly reduced the achievement gap between black and white children? Have income disparities withered away? Can we even say that schools are less segregated than they were 50 years ago? This is not a lesson that attempts to analyze the ambiguous legacy of desegregation. Instead it celebrates the determination and sacrifice of those individuals who were the shock troops in this struggle. And, to a lesser extent, it attempts to examine some of the resistance to school integration. Students watch the video, but through writing they are also invited to "become" the individuals whose lives shaped and were shaped by these key civil rights battles.

Materials Needed:

- Video: *Eyes on the Prize:* "Fighting Back: 1957-1962;" Optional: copies of the Student Handouts: "Inside Elizabeth Ann Eckford;" and "In Their Own Words: *Eyes on the Prize:* Little Rock and Mississippi."

- [Optional.] A transcript of this episode of *Eyes on the Prize* can be found online at: http://www.pbs.org/wgbh/amex/eyesonthe prize/about/pt_102.html.

Suggested Procedure:

1. Explain to students that you'll be asking them to do some writing based on the events depicted in the video they're about to view. They'll have the choice of writing interior monologues, stories, poems, dialogue (two-voice) poems, diary entries, or letters. Ask them to write down incidents during the video that they find especially sad, inspiring, or outrageous. They might write their impressions of particular characters or events. Urge them to "steal" lines from the narrator or people interviewed. They'll be able to incorporate these in their writing.

2. Show the video. Over the years I've supervised a number of student teachers. It's interesting to watch how some of them use video in the classroom. At least initially, their strategy is to wheel the VCR-DVD and television to the front of the classroom turn it on and go back to their desk to watch or grade papers. Needless to say, this does not always result in students' rapt attention and full comprehension. I'm an interventionist when it comes to showing videos. Particularly with documentaries, which often require more context-setting, I sit by the television and stop it frequently to ask a question or point something out. I may rewind it to

replay someone's comment or an especially poignant scene. At times, I pause it to ask students to wonder what might be going through a person's mind at a particular point or to anticipate how an individual or group will resolve a dilemma. I try not to overdo it, and I have to confess that, at least at first, some students are annoyed by this practice. They have years of video-watching practice—staring at the screen—and don't feel that they need someone butting in to ask questions and make them mentally "talk back" and evaluate underlying messages. Generally, we reach a kind of negotiated middleground—somewhere between their desire to be left alone to enjoy or "veg-out" and my desire ask them to think about every last nuance.

3. Stop the video immediately after Elizabeth Eckford (one of the nine students chosen to desegregate Little Rock's Central High School) gets on the bus. Read aloud the dramatic account excerpted from NAACP leader Daisy Bates' *The Long Shadow of Little Rock*, included here as the Student Handout, "Inside Elizabeth Ann Eckford."

4. Resume the video.

5. Some questions for discussion afterwards:

   • The narrator in the video comments that because other forms of integration had been successful in Little Rock, some people hoped that the same would be true for school integration. Why wasn't this the case?

   • Why did President Eisenhower not act sooner to force Governor Faubus to allow the nine students into Central High School?

   • Eisenhower sends in the troops to protect the "Little Rock Nine." The *Eyes on the Prize* narrator comments, "The troops did not, however, mean the end of harassment; it meant the declaration of war." Who were the sides in this war? What were they fighting for?

   • Melba Pattillo Beals describes how she was tripped and fell onto broken glass. Why did the black students put up with all the abuse? Why not just say, "Forget it. I'm leaving"?

   • Look at the comments by the white student about Spanish and Chinese people on the "In Their Own Words" handout. When she declares that Negroes are "more different" than Spanish people, what do you think she's referring to?

   • Why does Melba burn her books?

   • Constance Baker Motley says that the Civil Rights struggles in the South created a "genuine revolution on the part of black people." Do you agree? How do you define "revolution"? What were the aims of this revolution?

   • Analyze the Ross Barnett quote from his speech at the Mississippi-Kentucky football game. Who are the "people" he refers to? What are their "customs" and "heritage"?

   • The reporter asks James Meredith if he felt guilty for the deaths at Ole Miss. Should Meredith have felt guilty? If Meredith hadn't been so diplomatic, how might he have responded?

6. Ask students to write from the video. One option is to postpone a discussion of the video until after students have written, and then to incorporate the above questions into a discussion that grows out of the writing. Allow students to choose how they respond to the video: interior monologues, stories, poems, dialogue poems, diary entries, or letters. Brainstorm possible topics with students. For example, they might write as James Meredith when the reporter asks him if he feels guilty; as Ernest Green when he walks across the stage to accept his diploma; as Melba watching her books burn; as Minnie Jean when she dumps chili on the head of the white boy who harassed her; as the all-black cafeteria workers watching and applauding. Students could write dialogue poems from

Whites harass Elizabeth Ann Eckford, one of nine African American students attempting to begin the 1957-58 school year at Little Rock's Central High School.

the standpoint of black and white students in Central High School. [For examples, see "Two Women" in *Rethinking Our Classrooms, Vol. 1* or "Two Young Women" in *Rethinking Globalization*]:

> I am a student
> **I am a student ...**

Or students could write dialogue poems from the standpoint of white and black reporters about any of the events depicted in the video.

List students' writing ideas on the board. Encourage them to choose the form of writing that will best allow them to explore the emotions and ideas they had during the video. I always make sure to give students time to begin—if not finish—the writing in class, as I find that this results in students producing more and better quality papers.

7. Seat students in a circle and invite them to share their pieces in a read-around. Ask them to be alert to common themes in their writing. In my classes, some students focus on the hardships of the African American teenagers attempting to integrate Central High School, as does Lila Johnson in her poem:

> *I remember the mob*
> *how faces became blurred shades*
> *of light and dark*
> *how fingers reached greedily for*
> *a sleeve an arm a neck*
> *how bodies formed*
> *an intricate weave*
> *and squeezed*
> *in hopes of crushing*
> *a young black girl*

Frequently, students write from Melba Pattillo Beals' standpoint [see Linda Christensen's article in *Rethinking Schools*, Vol. 18 #3, "Warriors Don't Cry: Brown Comes to Little Rock"] as she burns her books after that 1957-58 school year. Sarah Sherwood penned a bitter piece she called "The Fire in My Soul:"

> *I swore to myself I would never go back there*
> *again, that I would never put myself through*
> *that kind of humiliation again. I hated them;*

Eight of the nine black students walk to their waiting Army station wagon, Oct. 2, 1957.

I hated them for making me hate. I told myself I would never become like them, but here I am wishing they were all dead.

And then she lights her books on fire:

I sat there and watched as my dreams, my hopes, burned away. I coldly stared at the flame. There were no more tears to cry.

Despite the anguish in students' writing, perhaps the most common motif in their pieces is defiance. Alice Ramos imagines the thoughts of Ernest Green, the first African American to graduate from Central High School:

But I graduated from
your all-white, all-prejudice school

They didn't clap
When I went to pick up my diploma

But I didn't care
I don't need their clapping

I beat the monster
that day I stepped inside the school.

In fact, more than 50 years after *Brown*, we can see that the "monster" is more multifaceted, more complicated than it may have appeared to the NAACP activists who led the move to integrate Little Rock's Central High School. So we need to help our students reflect on alternatives that Civil Rights activists might have pursued 50 years ago, and let's help students probe the contemporary nature of the monster of racial inequality. But we can also offer students the opportunity to celebrate the courage and tenacity of the young people who risked their lives for a better education—for themselves and for those who would come after. ◼

This article first appeared in a special edition of Rethinking Schools *magazine, "The Promise," on the 50th anniversary of the Supreme Court's* Brown v. Board *decision (Spring 2004; Vol. 18, #3).*

Inside Elizabeth Ann Eckford

THAT NIGHT I WAS SO EXCITED I couldn't sleep. The next morning I was about the first one up. While I was pressing my black-and-white dress—I had made it to wear on the first day of school—my little brother turned on the TV set. They started telling about a large crowd gathered at the school. The man on TV said he wondered if we were going to show up that morning. Mother called from the kitchen, where she was fixing breakfast, "Turn that TV off!" She was so upset and worried. I wanted to comfort her, so I said, "Mother, don't worry."

Elizabeth Ann Eckford

AP Images

Dad was walking back and forth, from room to room, with a sad expression. He was chewing on his pipe and he had a cigar in his hand, but he didn't light either one. It would have been funny only he was so nervous.

Before I left home Mother called us into the living room. She said we should have a word of prayer. Then I caught the bus and got off a block from the school. I saw a large crowd of people standing across the street from the soldiers guarding Central. ...

[Little Rock School] Superintendent Blossom had told us to enter by the front door. I looked at all the people and thought, "Maybe I will be safer if I walk down the block to the front entrance behind the guards."

At the corner I tried to pass through the long line of guards around the school so as to enter the grounds behind them. One of the guards pointed across the street. So I pointed in the same direction and asked whether he meant for me to cross the street and walk down. He nodded "yes." So, I walked across the street conscious of the crowd that stood there, but they moved away from me.

For a moment all I could hear was the shuffling of their feet. Then, someone shouted.

"Here she comes, get ready!" I moved away from the crowd on the sidewalk and into the street. If the mob came at me I could then cross back over so the guards could protect me.

The crowd moved in closer and then began to follow me, calling me names. I still wasn't afraid. Just a little bit nervous. Then my knees started to shake all of a sudden and I wondered whether I could make it to the center entrance a block away. It was the longest block I ever walked in my whole life.

Even so, I still wasn't too scared because all the time I kept thinking that the guards would protect me.

When I got right in front of the school, I went up to a guard again. But this time he just looked straight ahead and didn't move to let me pass him. I didn't know what to do. Then I looked and saw that the path leading to the front entrance was a little farther ahead. So I walked until I was right in front of the path to the front door.

I stood looking at the school—it looked so big! Just then the guards let some white students go through.

The crowd was quiet. I guess they were waiting to see what was going to happen. When I was able to steady my knees, I walked up to the guard who had let the white students in. He too didn't move. When I tried to squeeze past him, he raised his bayonet and then the other guards closed in and they raised their bayonets.

They glared at me with a mean look and I was very frightened and didn't know what to do. I turned around and the crowd came toward me.

They moved closer and closer. Somebody started yelling, "Lynch her! Lynch her!"

I tried to see a friendly face somewhere in the mob—someone who maybe would help. I looked into the face of an old woman and it seemed a kind face, but when I looked at her again, she spat on me.

They came closer, shouting, "No nigger bitch is going to get in our school. Get out of here!"

I turned back to the guards but their faces told me I wouldn't get help from them. Then I looked down the block and saw a bench at the bus stop. I thought, "If I can only get there I will be safe." I don't know why the bench seemed a safe place to me, but I started walking toward it. I tried to close my mind to what they were shouting, and kept saying to myself, "If I can only make it to the bench I will be safe."

When I finally got there, I don't think I could have gone another step. I sat down and the mob crowded up and began shouting all over again. Someone hollered, "Drag her over to this tree! Let's take care of the nigger." Just then a white man sat down beside me, put his arm around me and patted my shoulder. He raised my chin and said, "Don't let them see you cry."

Then, a white lady—she was very nice—she came over to me on the bench. She spoke to me but I don't remember now what she said. She put me on the bus and sat next to me. She asked me my name and tried to talk to me but I don't think I answered. I can't remember much about the bus ride, but the next thing I remember I was standing in front of the School for the Blind, where Mother works.

I thought, "Maybe she isn't here. But she has to be here!" So I ran upstairs, and I think some teachers tried to talk to me, but I kept running until I reached Mother's classroom.

Mother was standing at the window with her head bowed, but she must have sensed I was there because she turned around. She looked as if she had been crying, and I wanted to tell her I was all right. But I couldn't speak. She put her arms around me and I cried. ∎

From Daisy Bates, The Long Shadow of Little Rock. *(New York: David McKay, 1962).*

In Their Own Words

Eyes on the Prize:
Little Rock and Mississippi

Melba Pattillo Beals: "The mob was getting past the wooden saw horses, because the policemen would no longer fight their own in order to protect us. And so someone made the suggestion that if they allowed the mob to hang one kid they could then get the rest out. And a gentleman whom I believed to be the assistant Chief of Police said, 'How you gonna choose? You gonna let them draw straws?'"

Ernest Green, on the black students' first trip to Central High with federal troops: "Well, we got into the jeep, into the stationwagon, rather. And the convoy that went from Mrs. Bates' house to the school had a jeep in front, a jeep behind. They both had machine gun mounts. And then the whole school was ringed with paratroopers and helicopters hovering around. We marched up the steps in this circle of soldiers with bayonets drawn. I figured that we had really gone into school that day. And walking up the steps that day was probably one of the biggest feelings I've ever had. I figured I'd finally cracked it."

Melba Pattillo Beals: "You'd be walking out to the volleyball court, and someone would break a bottle and trip you on the bottle. I have scars on my right knee from that."

White reporter to white high school student: "Do you think you'll get used to going to school with colored children?"

White student: "Yes, sir. I think so. I mean if I'm gonna have to do it I might as well get used to it."

White student: "If a Spanish or a Chinese person come here it wouldn't be hard to get along with them. It's just that the Negroes are what you might say, more different to us than a Spanish person might be."

Melba Pattillo Beals: "By the time school had ended I had sort of settled into myself. And I could have gone on for the next five years—it didn't matter anymore. I was past feeling. I was into just that kind of numb pain where you say, 'Hey, I can make it. Do whatever you'd like, and it just doesn't matter anymore.' But I came home and by myself I walked to the back yard and I burned my books, and I burned everything that I could burn. And I just stood there crying looking into the fire. And wondering whether I would go back, but not wanting to go back."

Constance Baker Motley: "It was a genuine revolution on the part of black people."

White student, Ole Miss: "If the school is closed, we want the (football) games played anyway."

Ross Barnett, Governor of Mississippi, at Mississippi-Kentucky football game: "I love Mississippi. I love her people, our customs. I love and respect our heritage."

Burke Marshall, Assistant U.S. Attorney General: "In a way, Oxford had become the symbol of massive resistance in the final gasp of the Civil War."

White reporter to James Meredith after the riots and deaths at the University of Mississippi: "Sir, there's been a great deal of turmoil and conflict. Two people have been killed. Do you have any feelings of guilt? Have you given it any second thoughts?" ■

Whose "Terrorism"?

SHORTLY AFTER THE SEPTEMBER 11 ATTACKS on the World Trade Center and the Pentagon, President George W. Bush announced these as acts of war, and proclaimed a "war on terrorism." But what exactly was to be the target of this war? And what precisely did the president mean by terrorism? Despite uttering the words "terror," "terrorist," or "terrorism" 32 times in his September 20 speech to the nation, he never defined terrorism.

Teachers need to engage our students in a deep critical reading of terms—such as "terrorism," "freedom," "patriotism," and "our way of life"—that evoke vivid images but can be used for ambiguous ends.

Lesson on Terrorism

I wanted to design a lesson that would get students to surface the definitions of terrorism that they carry around—albeit most likely unconsciously. And I wanted them to apply their definitions to a number of episodes, historical and contemporary, which involved some kind of violence or destruction. I didn't know for certain, but my hunch was that as students applied definitions consistently, they might be able to call into question the "We're Good/They're Bad" dichotomies that have become even more pronounced on the political landscape.

So I wrote up several "What Is Terrorism?" scenarios, but instead of using the actual names of countries involved, I substituted fictional names. Given the widespread conflation of patriotism with support for U.S. government policies, I had no confidence that students

Women watch the World Trade Center burn.

AP Images/Ernesto Mora

would be able to label an action taken by their government as "terrorism" unless I attached pseudonyms to each country.

In the following scenario I used the example of U.S. support for the Nicaraguan Contras in the 1980s. Tobian is the United States; Ambar is Nicaragua, and the country next door is Honduras:

The Tobian government is very unhappy with the government of Ambar, whose leaders came to power in a revolution that threw out the former Ambar dictator. Tobian decides to overthrow the new Ambar leaders. It begins funding a guerrilla army that attacks Ambar from another country next door. Tobian also builds army bases in the next-door country and allows the guerrilla army to use these bases. Tobian supplies almost all of the weapons and equipment of the guerrilla army fighting Ambar. The guerrillas generally try to avoid fighting Ambar's army. Instead, they attack clinics, schools, and cooperative farms. Sometimes they mine the roads. Tobian-supported guerrillas kill and maim many, many civilians. The guerrillas raid Ambar and then retreat into the country next door where Tobian has military bases.

Question:

1. **Which, if any, of these activities should be considered "terrorism" according to your definition?**

2. **Who are the "terrorists"?**

3. **What more would you need to know to be more sure of your answer?**

I knew that in such compressed scenarios lots of important details would be missing; hence, I included question number three to invite students to consider other details that might influence their decisions.

Other scenarios included Israeli soldiers taunting and shooting children in Palestinian refugee camps, with the assistance of U.S. military aid; Indian farmers burning Monsanto-supplied, genetically-modified cotton crops and threatening to destroy Monsanto offices; the 1998 U.S. cruise missile attack on Sudan's main pharmaceutical plant; and sanctions against Iraq that according to the U.N. reports killed as many as a half million children. I wasn't aiming to prejudge any of these as "terrorist," but I hoped that the diversity of examples would prompt students to wrestle with the concept.

Defining Terrorism

As I was on a leave of absence, my colleague, Sandra Childs, invited me into her Franklin High School classroom to teach this lesson to her 11th-grade Global Studies students. I began by asking students to write down their own personal definitions of terrorism, and to keep these questions in mind: Does terrorism need to involve the killing of many people or can it affect just one person?

An Afghan funeral service for a 20-year-old woman killed by U.S. bombing north of Kabul.

Can it involve simply the destruction of property, with no injuries? Can governments commit acts of terrorism, or is the term reserved only for people who operate outside of governments? Must terrorism involve the people of one country attacking citizens of another country? Does motive make a difference? Does terrorism need to be intentional?

Immediately following, I explained to students that, in preparation for an activity, I'd like them to get into small groups and read their individual definitions to one another to see if they could build a consensus definition of terrorism. They could choose an exemplary definition from one member or, if they preferred, cobble one together from their separate definitions.

Some groups quickly agreed upon definitions; others would have spent the entire 83-minute class debating definitions if Sandra and I had let them. In most cases, the definitions were simple, but thoughtful. For example: "Intentional acts that create terror, targeted towards a specific group, or innocent people. Not just directly, but indirectly."

I distributed the "What Is Terrorism?" scenarios to students, reviewed the instructions with them, and emphasized that all the scenarios were real. Their task was to read each situation and to decide whether any of the actions described met their group's definition of "terrorism." I gave them permission to approach the situations in whatever order they liked.

Watching students attempt to apply their definitions of terrorism, I was impressed by their eagerness to be consistent. As Sandra and I wandered from group to group, we heard students arguing over whether there was a distinction between oppression and terrorism. Most groups wanted more information on the motives of various actors. Some insisted that if a country supported terrorist acts in another country, then it too was a terrorist; others held that a supporting country could not be held fully responsible for the actions of the actual perpetrators—but if a country knew about terrorism enabled with its funds, and did nothing to prevent it, then it too could be considered guilty of terrorism.

Although this activity was far too involved to be neatly contained in an 83-minute class, by the end many students came to important insights. One student said, "Ever since they announced that we were going to have a war on terrorism I have wondered who or what a terrorist is. And ... it's suspicious that they still haven't defined terrorism." I asked students why they thought the U.S. government had failed to offer a clear definition of terrorism. One student said, "If you don't have any boundaries, then anyone can be a terrorist." Another said, "The U.S. government won't define terrorism because they don't want to be able to be considered terrorists."

These comments echoed Pakistani scholar and activist Eqbal Ahmad's insight that countries that have no intention of being consistent will resist defining terms. ["Terrorism: Theirs and Ours," a speech by Eqbal Ahmad at the University of Colorado, Boulder, Oct. 12, 1998.] As one student wrote after the activity: "I also realized how many terrorism acts the U.S. has committed. When our government doesn't define terrorism, it makes me think that they just want a free shot to kill anyone they want." Wrote another student: "Bush needs to define terrorism in front of our nation before he does anything else, and then he needs to stick with the definition, not bend it to suit the U.S."

But then there was this student comment: "I, myself, am really tired of hearing about it. If I go to war, so what, I'll fight for my country. What does this have to do with global studies?" And this young man: "I feel if we don't get our revenge against these 'terrorists' it will diminish the trust of our nation towards our government."

These remarks reminded me of being in the classroom during the fall of 1990, after Iraq had invaded Kuwait and the United States was assembling its military attack force. Many students resisted critical analysis, sensing that critique eroded the "patriotic" unity then building in the country—that appending a "not so fast" onto the flag-waving interrupted a sense of collective purpose that felt good to many of them. At least that was how I read some students' resistance. During times of war, students may regard even the mildest critical examination of government policy as unpatriotic or even subversive. Nonetheless, I was impressed by how many students in Sandra's

"Truth and Justice." Relatives of victims who disappeared during the 1973-90 dictatorship of Gen. Augusto Pinochet in Santiago, Chile.

classes appeared eager to question their government's framing of key issues.

As we wrapped up in one class, Sandra asked a wonderful question: "What difference do you think it would make if students all over the country were having the discussion that we're having today?"

There were two quick answers before the bell rang: "I'd feel a lot better about the U.S.," and "I think we'd lose a lot of people who'd want to go fight for the country."

My interpretation: The more students understand about the exercise of U.S. power in the world—both military and economic—the less likely they are to want to extend it.

Economic Terrorism

After I'd used the "What Is Terrorism?" situations with Sandra's classes, I realized that, with the exception of sanctions, all of them were incidents of direct attacks on civilians or property. Did my examples narrow students' consideration of "terrorism"?

In her article "Solidarity Against All Forms of Terrorism," Indian environmentalist and scholar Vandana Shiva urges us to embrace a more expansive notion of terrorism. She asks us to consider "economic policies which push people into poverty and starvation as a form of terrorism," such as International Monetary Fund/World Bank-mandated structural adjustment programs that force governments to cut food and medical programs, with the full knowledge of the misery this will engender. In India, Shiva writes:

Fifty million tribals who have been flooded out of their homes by dams over the past four decades were also victims of terrorism—they have faced the terror of technology and destructive development. The whole world repeatedly watched the destruction of the World Trade Center towers, but the destruction of millions of sacred shrines and homes and farms by forces of injustice, greed, and globalization go unnoticed.

To help students consider whether some situations could be considered economic terrorism, I've added several new "What Is Terrorism?" scenarios. One deals with deaths in southern Africa from AIDS, where, for instance, international banks have forced the Zambian government to pay annual debt service charges greater than spending on health and education combined and where, according to the United Nations, life expectancy will soon drop to 33 years, a level not seen in the Western world since medieval times. Another new

Two men carry children blinded by the Union Carbide chemical pesticide leak to a hospital in Bhopal, India, Dec. 5, 1984.

scenario focuses on transnational corporations that knowingly pay wages that are insufficient to sustain life.

Terrorism's Ghosts

The U.S. government is ill-placed to lecture the world about terrorism, especially when it has never bothered to define it. Writing in the British daily *The Guardian,* Indian novelist Arundhati Roy offered the perspective of an individual who is on the receiving end of U.S. global power:

> *The Sept. 11 attacks were a monstrous calling card from a world gone horribly wrong. The message may have been written by bin Laden (who knows?) and delivered by his couriers, but it could well have been signed by the ghosts of the victims of America's old wars. The millions killed in Korea, Vietnam and Cambodia, the 17,500 killed when Israel— backed by the U.S.—invaded Lebanon in 1982, the 200,000 Iraqis killed in Operation Desert Storm, the thousands of Palestinians who have died fighting Israel's occupation of the West Bank. And the millions who died, in Yugoslavia, Somalia, Haiti, Chile, Nicaragua, El Salvador, the Dominican Republic, Panama, at the hands of all the terrorists, dictators and genocidists whom the American government supported, trained, bankrolled and supplied with arms. And this is far from being a comprehensive list.*

It's not our role as teachers to climb on our soapbox to rail about U.S. foreign policy. And yet without an honest examination of events like those listed by Roy, how can we expect students to maintain any critical perspective on the U.S. "war against terrorism"? Let's clarify with students what precisely we mean by terrorism. And then let's encourage students to apply this definition to U.S. conduct in the world.

Underlying this curricular demand for consistency is the basic democratic, indeed human, premise that the lives of people from one nation are not worth more than the lives of people from another. A Pakistani university student, Nabil Ahmed, expressed this sentiment to the *Christian Science Monitor:* "There is only one way for America to be a friend of Islam. And that is if they consider our lives to be as precious as their own." ■

This is adapted from the Rethinking Schools book Whose Wars? Teaching About the Iraq War and the War on Terrorism.

What Is Terrorism?
Who Are the Terrorists?

Instructions:

Based on the definitions of terrorism that your group came up with, decide:

1. Which of the situations below are "terrorism";

2. Who are the "terrorists" in the situation; and

3. What additional information you would need to know to be more sure of your answers.

All the situations below are true, but the names of countries and peoples have been changed. It may help your group to make a diagram of some of the situations.

Situations:

1. Soldiers from the country of Marak surround a refugee camp made up of people from the country of Bragan. The refugee camp is crowded and the people there are extremely poor. Most of the Bragan people in the refugee camp hate the Marak army, believing that Marak has invaded Bragan, has taken all the best land and resources for themselves, and treats people from Bragan very poorly. Young men in the refugee camp sometimes fire guns at the soldiers.

   According to an eyewitness, a reporter from the *New York Times*, Marak soldiers use loudspeakers to call insults into the refugee camp—in the Bragan language. Over the loudspeakers, soldiers shout obscenities and things like, "Son of a whore!" They dare Bragan boys to come out near the electric fence that separates the refugee camp from a wealthy settlement of Marak citizens. When the boys—sometimes as young as 10 or 11—and young men go near the fence to throw stones or yell at the Marak soldiers, the soldiers use silencers and fire on the boys with live ammunition, often killing or maiming them. In an article, the *New York Times* reporter expressed horror at what he witnessed. He wrote: "Children have been shot in other conflicts I have covered—death squads gunned them down in El Salvador and Guatemala, mothers with infants were lined up and massacred in Algeria, and Serb snipers put children in their sights and watched them crumple onto the pavement in Sarajevo—but I have never before watched soldiers entice children like mice into a trap and murder them for sport." The Marak government clearly knows about the behavior of their soldiers and does nothing to stop them. Indeed, Marak soldiers so regularly taunt Bragan citizens that this behavior appears to be the policy of the Marak government. One additional fact: Every year, Marak is given enormous amounts of money and military equipment by the country of Bolaire, which is aware of how these are used by Marak.

2. Farmers from the country of Belveron are angry at their own government and at a corporation from the country of Paradar. The Belveron government has allowed the Paradar corporation to plant "test" crops of genetically-engineered cotton. The genetically-engineered crops produce their own pesticide. Many Belveron farmers worry that

the genetically-engineered crops will pollute their crops—as has happened many times in other countries—and will lead to a breed of super-pests that will be immune to chemical pesticides and also to the organic pest control methods many poor farmers use. Without growing and selling cotton, the farmers have no way to feed their families. Belveron farmers also believe that the Paradar corporation does not really care about them, but they instead care only for their own profit. They believe that the corporation wants to get Belveron farmers "addicted" to genetically-engineered cotton seeds—which the corporation has patented—so that the corporation will have a monopoly. Belveron farmers further point out that the corporation has not told farmers that the "tests" on their land may be risky, and could pollute their non-genetically-engineered cotton crops.

Belveron farmers have announced that they will burn to the ground all the genetically-engineered cotton crops. They hope to drive the Paradar corporation out of Belveron. Belveron farmers have also threatened that they may destroy the offices of the Paradar corporation.

3. The Kalimo army has invaded the country of Iona, next door. There are a number of refugee camps in Iona with thousands of people living in them. The refugees themselves lost their homes many years before—some in wars with Kalimo, others were forced out of their homes by Kalimo. The area around the refugee camps is controlled by the Kalimo army. The commander of the Kalimo army sealed off the refugee camps and allowed militias from Iona, who are hostile to the refugees, to enter two refugee camps and slaughter hundreds of people. The killing went on for 40 hours. At least 1,800 people were murdered, perhaps more. One additional fact: The Kalimo army receives a great deal of military aid from the country of Terramar. Terramar learned of the massacre of the refugees in Iona, but did not stop military aid to Kalimo.

4. A corporation based in the country of Menin has a chemical factory located in the much poorer country of Pungor. One night, huge amounts of poisonous gases from the factory begin spewing out into the area around the factory. Nobody outside the factory was warned because someone in the company had turned off the safety siren. Not until the gas was upon residents in their beds, searing their eyes, filling their mouths and lungs, did the communities surrounding the factory know of their danger. According to one report: "Gasping for breath and near blind, people stampeded into narrow alleys. In the mayhem children were torn from the hands of their mothers, never to see them again. Those who still could were screaming. Some were racked with seizures and fell under trampling feet. Some, stumbling in a sea of gas, their lungs on fire, were drowned in their own bodily fluids." No one knows how many people died, but perhaps as many as 6,000 that night and in the years after, more than 10,000.

The corporation had begun a cost-cutting drive prior to the disaster: lowering training periods for operatives, using low-cost materials, adopting hazardous operating procedures, cutting the number of operatives in half. A confidential company audit prior to the accident had identified 61 hazards. Nothing was done.

After the tragedy, the corporation concentrated on avoiding liability, sending in its legal team days before a medical team. Company officials lied about the poisonous nature of the chemicals at the plant. To this day the corporation refuses to disclose medical information on the leaked gases, maintaining it to be a "trade secret." The company did pay some of the victims' families. On average, victims received less than $350 from the company—a total loss of 48 cents per share of company stock.

Today, conditions in this Pungor community are hazardous: soil and water are still heavily contaminated. Mercury has been found at between 20,000 and six million times the expected levels. In this community, the rate of stillborn infants is three times the national average of Pungor; infant mortality is twice as high as the national average.

5. The Tobian government is very unhappy with the government of Ambar, whose leaders came to power in a revolution that threw out the former Ambar dictator. Tobian decides to overthrow the new Ambar leaders. It begins funding a guerrilla army that attacks Ambar from another country next door. Tobian also builds army bases in the next-door country and allows the guerrilla army to use these bases. Tobian supplies almost all of the weapons and equipment of the guerrilla army fighting Ambar. The guerrillas generally try to avoid fighting Ambar's army. Instead, they attack clinics, schools, and cooperative farms. Sometimes they mine the roads. Tobian-supported guerrillas kill and maim many, many civilians. The guerrillas raid Ambar and then retreat into the country next door where Tobian has military bases.

6. Simultaneously, the embassies of the country of Anza in two other countries were bombed. In one country, 213 people were killed and over 1,000 injured; in the other, 11 people were killed and at least 70 injured. In retaliation, about three weeks later, Anza launched missiles at the capital city of Baltus, destroying a pharmaceutical factory and injuring at least 10 people, and killing one. Anza claimed that this factory was manufacturing chemicals that could be used to make VX nerve gas—although Anza offered no substantial proof of this claim. Anza also claimed that a prominent individual whom they link to the embassy bombings was connected to the pharmaceutical factory, although they provided no evidence of this claim, either—and a great deal of evidence exists to prove that there is no link. Baltus pointed out that two years earlier they expelled the prominent individual, and vigorously denied that the pharmaceutical plant was producing nerve gas agents. They

said that this was an important factory, producing 70 percent of the needed medicines for the people of Baltus—including vital medicines to treat malaria and tuberculosis. They allowed journalists and other diplomats to visit the factory to verify that no chemical weapons were being produced there. Journalists and others who visited the factory agreed that the destroyed factory appeared to be producing only medicines. It is not known how many people may have died in Baltus for lack of the medicines that were being produced in that factory. Anza blocked the United Nations from launching the investigation demanded by Baltus.

7. At least one million people in the country of Lukin are infected with HIV/AIDS. Between 1991 and 2001, 700,000 people died of AIDS in Lukin. Currently, about 300 people die each day of AIDS-related causes. Largely because of the HIV/AIDS crisis, life expectancy in Lukin is expected to drop from 43 to 33 years, a level last experienced in Europe in medieval times. AIDS could be controlled with a combination of drugs, frequently called a drug "cocktail," including AZT. However, given current drug prices, this could cost as much as $18,000 a year per patient.

This year, Lukin will pay $174 million in interest payments on its debt—most of which will go to two large international banks. This debt was incurred many years ago, by a different government than the current one. The loans were pushed by banks, which had huge amounts of money to lend because oil-producing countries had deposited so much of their revenue into these banks. As one observer put it, "The banks were hot to get in. All the banks ... stepped forward. They showed no foresight. They didn't do any credit analysis. It was wild."

Loans benefited mostly bankers and the rich of Lukin. However, most people in Lukin are poor—the gross national product (GNP) per capita is $350. The $174 million in interest payments is more than the money

Lukin will spend on health care and education combined. Money that could go to pay for AIDS prevention and therapies for people with AIDS instead is being sent to banks in so-called developed countries.

The international banks know about the dire health situation in Lukin. They have allowed Lukin to postpone some debts—but only after Lukin agreed to certain conditions set by the banks that gave the banks greater control over Lukin's economy, for example requiring Lukin to sell its national bank to private investors. Still, so long as the banks force Lukin to pay interest on its debts, there is no way Lukin can deal effectively with the AIDS crisis. Three hundred people a day continue to die.

8. Led by the country of Lomandia, the United Nations waged a war against the country of Moretta, saying that Moretta illegally invaded another nearby country. After Moretta's army was defeated and removed from the country they'd invaded, Lomandia pushed for "sanctions" against Moretta, until Moretta could prove that it was not engaged in a program to produce "weapons of mass destruction," like nuclear bombs or poison gas. The sanctions meant that Moretta was not allowed to buy or sell almost anything from other countries in the world. Moretta could not get spare parts to repair water purification plants damaged by bombing during the war. It could not get medicines and spare parts for medical equipment. Moretta claimed that it allowed inspections from the United Nations, but Lomandia says that it did not. Documents from Lomandia show that it knew that Moretta civilians were dying as a result of water-born diseases. When asked in a television interview about the reports of massive numbers of civilian deaths—perhaps as many as half a million children over several years—a high government official from Lomandia said: "I think that is a very hard choice, but the price, we think, the price is worth it."

9. Bartavia is considered by many to be one of the most repressive countries in the world,

especially if you are not white. Only whites can vote; only whites can travel freely; only whites can live where they like. Most whites live comfortably, even luxuriously. Conditions for people who are not white are some of the worst in the world. Bartavia imprisons people who organize for change. Torture is widespread and used by the Bartavia government against people working for equality. Over the years, there have been numerous massacres of non-white Bartavia civilians—sometimes of young children. The main organizations working for change in Bartavia have asked the world not to invest money in Bartavia and not to have economic or cultural relations with the country until it commits itself to change. Nonetheless, many countries continue to do business with Bartavia. One in particular, Sarino, has allowed its corporations to increase their investments in Bartavia from $150 million to $2.5 billion—all this during a period of tremendous violence and discrimination. Who knows how many thousands of people have been killed—through guns or poverty—as a result of Sarino's actions.

10. The Sport-King Corporation produces athletic equipment sold all over the world. Although the headquarters of Sport-King is in the country of Morcosas, all of its products are manufactured in other countries. Sport-King contracts with subcontractors to make its products. Over 500,000 people, mostly women, work for these subcontractors in poor countries.

Sport-King has a "Code of Conduct" which is supposed to ensure that workers are not mistreated by Sport-King's subcontractors. For example, no child laborers are supposed to be hired; no prisoners may be used as workers; workers may not be forced to work more than 60 hours a week, etc. Sport-King's "Code of Conduct" specifies that workers must be paid a country's "minimum wage." However, it does not say that this minimum wage needs to be a living wage. Even poor country governments admit that the minimum wage is not enough for people to live on. Sport-King says that it pays the legal wage, but it knows that not all its workers can survive on this wage.

Companies like Sport-King locate their factories in countries that don't allow unions, that outlaw strikes, and that jail workers who demand higher pay and better conditions. In fact, Sport-King chooses to locate its factories in some of the most repressive countries in the world. Human rights groups argue that companies like Sport-King knowingly locate their factories in repressive places so that workers can more easily be controlled and exploited. These human rights groups argue that companies like Sport-King could easily afford to pay their workers living wages, but because this would come out of their enormous profits they choose not to. ■

What Is Terrorism?
Who Are the Terrorists?

Who's who:

Situation 1:

Marak is Israel. Bragan is Palestine. Bolaire is the United States. This particular example is taken from "A Gaza Diary," by Chris Hedges in the October 2001 *Harpers*.

Situation 2:

Belveron is India. Paradar is the United States. The corporation is Monsanto.

Situation 3:

Kalimo is Israel. Iona is Lebanon. Terramar is the United States. The refugees are Palestinian. The camps were Sabra and Shatila in 1982. The militia was Christian Phalangist.

Situation 4:

Menin is the United States. Pungor is India. The corporation was Union Carbide, in Bhopal, India. The year was 1985.

Situation 5:

Tobian is the United States. Ambar is Nicaragua. The country next door is Honduras. The time is the 1980s during the U.S.-sponsored Contra war.

Situation 6:

Anza is the United States. Baltus is Sudan. The countries where the U.S. embassies were bombed are Kenya and Tanzania. The prominent individual mentioned is Osama bin Laden.

Situation 7:

Lukin is Zambia. The banks are the International Monetary Fund and the World Bank.

Situation 8:

Lomandia is the United States. Moretta is Iraq. The U.S. official quoted was then-U.S. Ambassador to the United Nations, later Secretary of State, Madeleine Albright on *60 Minutes*, interviewed by Leslie Stahl in 1996.

Situation 9:

Bartavia is South Africa during apartheid. Sarino is the United States.

Situation 10:

Sport-King is Nike, although it could be many transnational corporations. Morcosas is the United States.

About Howard Zinn

HOWARD ZINN GREW UP IN BROOKLYN in a working-class, immigrant household. At 18, he became a shipyard worker and three years later joined the Air Force. He flew bomber missions during World War II, after which he returned to Brooklyn.

Zinn went to college under the GI Bill and received his Ph.D. from Columbia University in history. He taught at Spelman College, where he served as an advisor to the Student Nonviolent Coordinating Committee (SNCC) and worked with young Civil Rights Movement activists including Alice Walker and Marian Wright Edelman. He was fired from Spelman for his support of the students. (He returned in 2005 to give the commencement address.)

Howard Zinn led antiwar protests, went to Vietnam with Daniel Berrigan, and testified in the Pentagon Papers trial of his friend, Daniel Ellsberg. He is the author of dozens of books, including the classic *A People's History of the United States* and *Declarations of Independence*. His essays have appeared in over 20 books; his plays include *Emma, Unsafe Distances,* and *Marx in Soho*.

Zinn's life was the subject of an award-winning documentary film narrated by actor Matt Damon, *Howard Zinn: You Can't Be Neutral on a Moving Train*.

Zinn lectured extensively across the United States as well as in Asia, Africa, and Europe. He was a visiting professor at the University of Paris and the University of Bologna, where he was a Fulbright Distinguished Professor.

Over his life, Howard Zinn won numerous awards including the Albert J. Beveridge Prize from the American Historical Association, the Thomas Merton Award, the Eugene V. Debs Award, the Upton Sinclair Award, the Lannan Literary Award, and the Havens Center Award for Lifetime Contribution to Critical Scholarship.

Howard Zinn died January 27, 2010 in the Los Angeles area at the age of 87. Obituaries and tributes to Zinn can be found at www.howardzinn.org, and in the Spring 2010 issue of *Rethinking Schools* magazine, www.rethinkingschools.org.

About Bill Bigelow

BILL BIGELOW HAS TAUGHT high school social studies in Portland, Ore., since 1978, and now works as an editor with *Rethinking Schools* magazine. He has authored or co-edited numerous books on teaching and learning, including *Strangers in Their Own Country: A Curriculum on South Africa* (Africa World Press), *The Power in Our Hands: A Curriculum on the History of Work and Workers in the United States* (Monthly Review Press), *Rethinking Columbus, Rethinking Our Classrooms: Vols. 1 and 2, Rethinking Globalization: Teaching for Justice in an Unjust World,* and *The Line Between Us: Teaching About the Border and Mexican Immigration* (all published by Rethinking Schools.) He lives in Portland, Ore. with his wife, Linda Christensen. He can be reached at bbpdx@aol.com.

TEACHING FOR CHANGE

The mission of Teaching for Change is to provide teachers and parents with the tools to transform schools into centers of justice where students learn to read, write and change the world. We do this through parent organizing, professional development and publications.

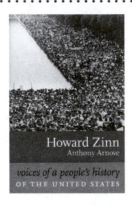

A PEOPLE'S HISTORY OF THE UNITED STATES: THE WALL CHARTS - $25

Illustrated timelines of over 500 years of US history. Booklet, 48 pp., + 2 posters, 13.75"x 9.5".

VOICES OF A PEOPLE'S HISTORY OF THE UNITED STATES - $19

Paralleling the 24 chapters of *A People's History of the United States* with first person voices. Paperback, 665 pp.

A YOUNG PEOPLE'S HISTORY OF THE UNITED STATES - $35

Excerpted from the full volume of *A People's History of the United States* to make it reader-friendly for middle school. 2 book set, Vol. I-212 pp., Vol II-234 pp.

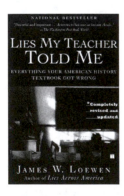

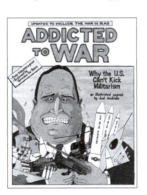

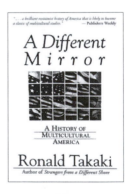

LIES MY TEACHER TOLD ME - $17

Everything Your American History Textbook Got Wrong
A thorough and essential critique of major US history high school textbooks. Paperback, 464 pp.

ADDICTED TO WAR - $10

Why the U.S. Can't Kick Militarism
A comic book explanation of why the U.S. has been in so many wars, who benefits, and who loses. Paperback, 78 pp.

A DIFFERENT MIRROR - $17

A History of Multicultural America
U.S. history through the experiences of Native Americans, African Americans, Jews, Irish Americans, Asian Americans, and Mexican-Americans. Paperback, 508 pp.

www.teachingforchange.org

People's History Classroom Resources

The Teaching for Change webstore offers hundreds of carefully selected books, films and posters for teaching from a social justice perspective. You can find these items—and much more—online at:
www.teachingforchange.org

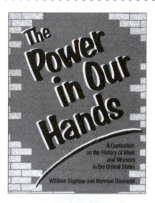

THE POWER IN OUR HANDS - $18

A Curriculum on the History of Work and Workers in the United States

Role plays and writing activities project students into real-life situations to explore the history and contemporary reality of employment (and unemployment) in the U.S. Paperback, 184 pp.

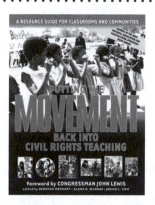

PUTTING THE MOVEMENT BACK INTO CIVIL RIGHTS TEACHING - $25

2004 NAME Award Winner

Readings and lessons for K-12 on the Civil Rights Movement, with an emphasis on the role of "ordinary people", women, youth, and related movements. Paperback, 576 pp. Published by Teaching for Change

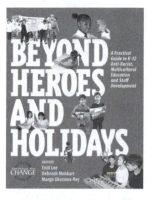

BEYOND HEROES AND HOLIDAYS - $35

A Practical Guide to K-12 Anti-Racist, Multicultural Education and Staff Development

The theory and practical examples for various grades and subjects on how to infuse a multicultural approach to all aspects of the school and classroom. Paperback, 432 pp. Published by Teaching for Change

MATEWAN DVD - $20

A feature film depicting a strike in a mining town in Appalachia and the struggle for solidarity across racial lines. 142 min.

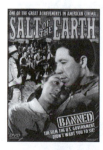

SALT OF THE EARTH DVD - $20

The struggle for equality of Mexican-American miners and their wives, based on an actual strike in New Mexico in 1951-52. B&W, 94 min.

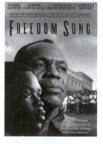

FREEDOM SONG DVD - $20

The story the Civil Rights Movement in Mississippi told through the voice of an African-American teenager. 117 min.

MADE IN L.A. DVD - $50

A moving documentary about how three women organize for fair labor rights in the apparel industry. 70 min.

When in the Washington, D.C. area, visit our bookstores located at Busboys and Poets
• FOOD • BOOKS • FILM • COFFEE • STAGE • INTERNET • BAR • WWW.BUSBOYSANDPOETS.COM •

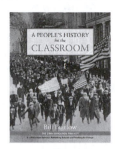
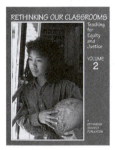
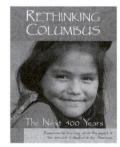
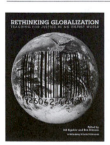